D1359623

HOW I CAN MAKE DECISIONS

BOOKS BY LAWRENCE O. RICHARDS

A New Face for the Church

Creative Bible Study

How I Can Be Real

How Far I Can Go

How I Can Experience God

How I Can Make Decisions

How I Can Fit In

69 Ways to Start a Study Group

Three Churches in Renewal

Reshaping Evangelical Higher Education
(with Marvin K. Mayers)

A Theology of Christian Education

A Theology of Church Leadership
(with Clyde Hoeldtke)

A Theology of Personal Ministry
(with Gib Martin)

Discipling Resources Series
(with Norman Wakefield)

ANSWERS FOR YOUTH SERIES

HOW I CAN MAKE DECISIONS

LARRY RICHARDS

Illustrations by Charles Shaw

ZONDERVAN
PUBLISHING HOUSE
OF THE ZONDERVAN CORPORATION
GRAND RAPIDS, MICHIGAN 49506

How I Can Make Decisions
Copyright © 1980 by The Zondervan Corporation

First published in 1970 by Moody Press, Chicago, under the title *What's In It For Me?* Copyright © 1970 by the Moody Bible Institute.

Fourth printing 1982

Library of Congress Cataloging in Publication Data

Richards, Lawrence O
    How I can make decisions.

    First ed. published in 1970 under title: What's in it for me?
    Includes bibliographical references.
    1. Youth—Religious life. I. Title.
BV4531.2.R454 1979   248'.83   79-16212
ISBN 0-310-38981-X

Unless otherwise indicated, Scripture quotations are taken from *The New Testament in Modern English,* © 1958 by J. B. Phillips.

Printed in the United States of America

Contents

1

Adrift

Ken glanced once at the Sunday bulletin, and then at his sister Carla. She was sitting straight and prim, apparently giving full attention to the service. Ken's pencil began to trace the letters on his bulletin, and to fill in spaces in the *p*'s and *b*'s and *o*'s.

He glanced up again when Pastor Black stepped up to the pulpit to begin his sermon. "Decision," the bulletin said, was the topic.

"Decisions," the pastor said, "are important to every one of us. Not just the big decisions people have to make, but the small ones too. In fact, what life holds for a person is largely up to us. The issues of life are in the choices we make daily. . . ."

Ken settled back and watched his pencil make more marks on the bulletin as he tuned out the message. *It's a nice idea,* he thought, *that people control their lives by their choices. Nice for adults. But how many decisions can a teen make? For Carla and me, life is mapped out by Mom and Dad, by school rules, and by what folks at church think kids ought* to do. *What chance do we have to make choices? Still, it would be nice to have some control over my life. Maybe someday—*

When we think about what we want out of life, and how we're going to get it, it's natural to think about the big decisions we make. Where am I going to college? Should I get a job instead? Whom am I going to marry? And when? What do I want for a career?

Such big decisions are important. They're turning points in any person's life.

But in this book I want to focus on *little* decisions—the kind of choices most of us may not even be conscious of.

What's so important about little decisions? Jan, now a college girl, sees it clearly: "In my high school years," she

shares, "I never went further than to think about where something would get me now, or how I could be popular now. When I finally realized that the choices I was making then were actually shaping me as a person, and the type of person I might always be, I realized I was making some big mistakes."[1] Youth, for Jan was a time adrift. She didn't think much about the choices she made. She just acted, and drifted along on the "now."

This feeling of being adrift is shared by a lot of young people. An Illinois girl says, "I can't remember any basic decisions in high school, actually. I just lived a day at a time, and did what seemed right and most fun at the time." Another adds, "It seems like some of my decisions were made for me—like where to go to church, and some things I 'shouldn't do.' And others—well, they just happened, and I gave little thought to them, even in college." For these two, life moved on, and they drifted with it.

Most of us feel adrift at times. Maybe the feeling has been deep down and we've hardly been aware of it. But at times we've wondered, *Now, why did I do that? Why did I act like that? Why did I make that choice?* Usually this wondering isn't pleasant. We think these thoughts when we're dissatisfied with ourselves, or something has made us feel a little wrong. Then we wish we had more control over ourselves and over our lives.

I think we *can* have more control, and this excites me. We can look closely at the little decisions we make, and discover how to take control rather than be controlled. We can discover how to choose the kind of person we're going to be, rather than be molded by the forces that push and pull us. All this can come when we look at the little decisions of life—and understand what's behind them.

Why the little decisions?

What is there in little decisions that make them so important? For one thing, the little decisions are the ones that, together, make up the pattern of your life. And it's the pattern that's important. It's the pattern, in a very real sense, that *is* you.

Look, for instance at Arlene and Tom. Each drifted through a series of little decisions into a pattern of life that deeply affected both of their personalities and characters. Each became unhappy about that way of life and made a real "take charge" decision, one that changed the pattern, and that changed each of them.

Arlene, a New Yorker, is a girl who was "in" and bothered about it. "As a freshman in high school I was confronted with the opportunity to pledge for the 'best' sorority of the neighborhood. Sororities and fraternities were the whole basis of the social structure of our school—you were either in or out, somebody or nobody. It was a super-organized secret society, but there were other Christians, nominal or otherwise, in it, and on the surface there didn't seem to be anything objectionable. I could rationally defend my decision before my other Christian friends, my Christian Ed. director (the one person I really didn't want to disappoint), and could almost convince myself and God that it was not contrary to His will. Once on the inside of the set, I had the opportunity to see the values of the group I had chosen to be a part of. It was entirely too obvious. I just could not ignore what the real motto was: Fun at anybody's expense. Actually, it was a little more sophisticated than that, but basically it was a security group where the security could be achieved only by destroying all outsiders—their happiness and their achievements. Once there was security, then there was all sorts of time for fun—moral or immoral—so long as it was fun. By the sophomore and junior year in a highly sophisticated subculture, sex is a delightful new toy. Now, not everyone felt this way. You could be in it but not of it, and there were a number of girls who were in this situation. But as a Christian I was aware of what this could do to my witness. Although I was doing nothing wrong, I was associating myself with it. I was compromising my values by my silence.

"Then there was the matter of time, which should have been better spent elsewhere. It was also interfering with other friendships which were more important to me, but I was required to spend a great deal of time with the sisters.

"After a year of this, and much more prayer than when I had to decide to pledge or not, God definitely laid it on my heart that this was not His will for my life, not the way He could use me most effectively. So then I had to go and speak to the president and explain my decision to drop out. I'm sure she never understood, and thought I was foolish, but God really gave me peace about it and filled my time with things that were more meaningful in His purpose.

"The fact was that my purposes and His purposes were meshing."

It was Tom, an Ohioan, who made a big deal out of a decision whether to win a race or not. He tells it like this:

"In high school track I would have been the hero of the team if I won the OVAC (Ohio Valley Athletic Conference) AA half-mile run. I was the favorite in the race, and none of the other runners had come within one second of my fastest time. Most of them ran a normal 2:08 half—I ran a 2:04 normally. I knew I could win; it would be easy. I would just run with the leader for the first lap, and pull away the second lap. But then I was faced with a value judgment—*should* I win?

"I know it may sound ridiculous, but I knew what would happen if I won. I would have a head so big it wouldn't fit through the school's double door. But I really wanted to be able to give God the credit. So the question was, Do I win it all by myself or do I ask God to make me finish second or third, or last—if my conceit was too great to take such a 'material' victory.

"I knew if I prayed about it I'd have to let God take over—so I did. You know, I was tied for first place with 175 yards to go in the race, and I felt like I could run all day. I was just ready to turn on the speed and leave the guy beside me, who was looking really tired anyway. But I blacked out—God blacked me out. The next thing I knew I was five feet from the finish line and directly behind the guy I was going to leave. Then it was over.

"I ran a 2:08.7, my slowest time by 1.2 seconds!

"Of course, the question comes up, Was it really a value judgment, or did I actually have no choice in the matter? For me, a junior in high school, it was a real value judgment, because I *knew* I could win it if I didn't pray, and simply ran my own race. (Whether I actually would have won or not doesn't matter. *I* was positive that I *could* win at the time.) But I decided that my serving God was more important, even if I did lose. Of course I wanted to win it, but I was willing to lose if God wanted me to. He took me up on it.

"I suppose that if I had to put the decision in terms of what values were weighed, I would say that I chose God over me; I chose to be humiliated before the other fellows on the squad rather than strut arrogantly in front of them and in the halls at school, glorifying me instead of glorifying God."

Now, why did I do that?

In including the stories of Arlene and Tom I'm not suggesting that there is anything inherently wrong about belonging to a sorority or winning a race. That's not the issue. What's really important is that these kids stopped drifting and looked seriously at their lives. Each looked at the pattern of his life and asked about his decisions, Now, why did I do *that*? Why have I acted as I have? Why have I made the choices I've made? What's behind the way I've been acting?

Stopping to ask is particularly important for anyone who has freedom to make any choices at all.

Sometimes high school guys or girls honestly feel they don't have even that freedom. Like Ken, a young person may feel that others map out life for him, and that he's just marking time until he finally leaves home and can begin to live on his own. But this really isn't true. Actually, teens have more freedom to make decisions and develop their own pattern of life today than most realize. One of the things I asked the guys and girls who helped write this book was What kind of choices do you have freedom to make? Here are some of their answers:

School activities I joined, courses I took, places I went.
Just minor ones, like whether or not to go to some meeting, to go to the movies, etc.
Whether or not to go out with the gang, to study or play basketball, or watch TV.
Moral decisions—I had to maintain my Christian standards with non-Christian friends.
Activities in and out of school; social activities in and out of church.
Choice of hobby; free-time uses; activities; dress.

Entertainment; whether or not to get a job.
How to act when I didn't get my way; places to go.
People to associate with; activities to participate in.
Social activities, entertainment, friends, relationships.
Fitting in—wearing clothes in fashion; what to do
    during the summer; daily routine; extra projects;
    doing things for others; whom to go out with; etc.

True, all these are just "little" decisions, the daily kind
anyone can make. But together they make up a great big
chunk of every teen's life, and they do point up broad
areas of freedom and responsibility. After all, when have
you seen a dad trail a son through school corridors, making decisions for him? "Don't talk to that kid." "Watch
your tone of voice there, son." "Now, go to study hall, not
off with the guys to talk." "Oops! Don't spend your lunch
money on that pinball machine."

Silly, isn't it? This sort of thing just doesn't happen. Not
today.

No, in most of your life, you're on your own.

And on your own you make the "little" decisions. They
may seem little, but woven all together they make up the
pattern of your life. The little decisions largely determine
the kind of person you're becoming, and what you're
going to get out of life.

It's because of this that we need to stop drifting early in
life, and raise questions of Why? Why do I make the decisions I make? Why do I choose what I choose?

Down underneath

"I valued my parents' respect and the respect of many of
my teachers," writes a young man from Illinois. "I had the
choice of being an everyday hood or I could try my best in
grades, athletics, etc. Because I valued other people's re-

spect, I chose not to be a hood. In doing this I lost respect from the hoods, but I figured it was worth it."

What this boy is saying is important. He's pointing out that his decisions weren't made just because he "liked" the things he chose. He didn't try for good grades because he liked A's and B's in themselves. Down underneath there was something important to him that good grades helped him gain. "I valued my parents' respect and the respect of many of my teachers." What was important to him was what these others thought about him. He made his daily decisions (about study, the use of his time, his choice of friends and activities) to gain and keep adult respect.

To another teen, what the "hoods" think might seem important, so he might choose not to study, not to discipline his use of time, not to avoid certain activities. For him too these daily decisions would have little to do with grades themselves. The reason he acts as he does is down underneath.

The down-underneath reasons for our behavior are called our *values,* and we're going to think a lot about values in this book. Understanding how values affect our decisions, and consciously *choosing our values,* is the key to becoming the kind of person we really want to be.

How important are values? The social sciences tell us that values underlie our pattern of life. These "What's important to me?" motives are reflected in the ways we act and the choices we make. Is your room a pigpen, or neat as the proverbial pin? Its condition can be traced to your values. What do you like to do on a date? What kind of clothes do you wear? What do you talk about with the gang? Whom do you choose as friends? How do you get along with mom and dad? Values again. All your habitual ways of doing things rest on values. Underneath all you do are the "What's important to me?" ideas you operate on.

The guy from Illinois I quoted recognized what value controlled his choice of behavior in school. But we don't have to be aware of our values to have them affect us. That's one of the biggest reasons why we need to think about the issues raised in this book. The Bible talks about drifting "along on the stream of this world's ideas of living" (Eph. 2:2), not even aware of the currents that control us. And it comes out strong for the idea that the Christian has to stop drifting, and to grab some oars.

To me, this is important. I don't want to be controlled by pushes and pulls from within that I'm not even aware of. I don't want to feel like a puppet on invisible strings. I really want more from life than that. Probably you do too. A young Pennsylvanian looks back unhappily on high school and early college and says, "I depended on what other people thought and didn't think for myself. I accepted advertisement persuasion and American middle-class values without questioning their true worth and durability. I didn't consider what was really important to me, and what I was doing right then that was best for me then and would be of value ten years later."

This is drifting.

And the way to stop drifting is to look at your values.

Steps to take

Reading this book will be more meaningful if you take time after each chapter to think, and to jot down answers to these questions. Why not try it?

1. List decisions Arlene and Tom might have made as a daily habit *before* they stopped to look at their

values. Then list several choices they might have made differently afterward.

2. Think back over yesterday, and jot down every choice you can remember making. (This might include use of time, use of money, ways you reacted to friends and family, etc.)
Do your choices tell you anything about your values?

3. In this chapter we've defined values as "What's important to me?" Make a list of what you believe is really important to you.

2

By probing

"Nobody makes a decision for no reason at all," writes a twenty-year-old from Paraguay. "Perhaps the issues are so cloudy in his own mind that a person does not know the reasons for making a certain choice, but a probing into that person's background, etc., will show why a decision was made."

"You kids are the most important thing in the world to me," gushed a mother with tears in her eyes. "Now shut up and let me watch this TV program."

A little ridiculous, isn't it? But it illustrates an important point. Our values are discovered by probing what we *do*, not by listening to what we say.

This is why I asked you to jot down that list of "what's important" in the last chapter—to help you discover if what you *think* is important to you, really *is*!

One writer says that values "consciously or unconsciously" are a "standard or criterion for guiding action."[1] That "consciously or unconsciously" is an important key to understanding ourselves and our values. We don't have to be aware of what's important to us for it to control our actions.

Take that mother. She *says* that her kids are the most important thing in the world to her, that, above all, she values their happiness and their good. And she probably believes it. But, how does she *act?* When it's a choice between listening to her kids or listening to TV, it's the kids she turns off!

Now, this may be just an isolated incident. Maybe the kids are nasty today, or she's feeling upset. But what if it's not an isolated incident? What if mom's normal response to her kids is "Shut up and leave me be!"? If this is the pattern of her relationship with her children, then we *know* that "what's important to her" is not the kids at all. Her behavior is a dead giveaway.

This is the way to test any person's values. Look at the pattern of his life and see what he does. And this is the way for you to discover your values. Check your pattern of life against what you *think* is important to you. If the two don't fit, the chances are you're controlled by one or more hidden values.

Hidden values are hard to dig out, even by probing. We can look at our life, but unless we understand some of the ways that hidden forces work, they may be hard to recognize in us.

So let's take a look at one common hidden value and see how it might gain control over a person's life.

Out of debt

"Tell the kids," says a fifteen-year-old guy from New Jersey, "not to let parents force them into the same job they have. And don't choose a job just for the money, but get a job you like. It would be no fun dreading each day of your working life."

Most would agree. This is the way a twenty-year-old college student puts it: "I don't have any trouble thinking of not having much materially if and when I serve as a missionary somewhere. As long as my wife and I have our necessities, and perhaps even if we don't, we'll be happy knowing that the Lord is with us, and we're in His work." If materialism means pinning our happiness on making money and having all the things money can buy, then these kids are out of debt. They don't owe their values to *that*.

Probably you feel a lot like they do. You wouldn't choose a job just because it offers a lot of money. You wouldn't spend your life piling up luxuries, and the idea of "not having much materially" may not bother you at all. Does that mean your values haven't been tainted by materialism? It might. But, then again, it might not.

For materialism isn't summed up in the number of things we own. It's related to our attitude toward material things in general.

Sometimes we can get spiritual values and material values all mixed up together. Like the twenty-year-old who wrote, "My reasons for choosing medical missions as a vocational goal: a chance to combine evangelization with humanitarian action, thus serving God while at the same time attaining a higher degree of security and status than other missions' vocations. These reasons entered into my decision-making in high school, and are still valid for me today." This guy recognizes, and freely admits, the role that security plays in his choices. His concern for serving God, he believes, led him to opt for missions. His desire for security and status led him to choose the kind of mission service to be in.

Really, it would be surprising if material possessions weren't important to us. We live in a very materialistic culture. Someone is always trying to convince us that we need something more, something new. Why trade in a car when it's a year old? Will the new car run better? No, but each year there's a new style—something to make the car look better to us. Somehow it makes Americans feel better—more important, more with it—if they ride in a new car rather than a year-old car. And "teenage values," say sociologists Grace and Fred Hechinger, "are invariably determined by the adult values around them."[2] If that's true, teenagers are going to value things highly because our whole culture, our whole adult world, places tremendous value on material things.

Jesus stated a simple principle that helps us evaluate.

When a man asked Him to force his brother to divide an estate, Jesus refused, saying that He had not been appointed to judge in that affair. Then, turning to His disciples, He said, "Notice that, and be on your guard against covetousness in any shape or form. For a man's real life in no way depends upon the number of his possessions" (Luke 12:15). According to this principle, covetousness (another way of saying "a controlling concern for things") can appear in a number of shapes and forms. And all of these are to be rejected because a man's real life does not *depend* on the number of his possessions. Now, how can life seem to depend on possessions?

In several ways.

One young high schooler broke down and cried when his parents had his hair cut shorter than he wanted. "I only had three things that made me different," he sobbed. "My hair, and now you've cut it. My jeans, and they're torn. Now all I've got left is my posters."

Somehow to this guy his hairdo, his clothes and his room decorations added up to *him*. His life seemed to depend on his possessions.

This attitude is materialism, pure and simple. It's not how much money you've got, or how much money you want. It's not how many things you've got, or how many more you want. *It's what your material possessions mean to you.*

A person's pattern of life may reveal in a number of ways that he actually is depending on things.

Take clothes. What do they mean to you?

Now, don't get me wrong. I don't think all Christians ought to go around in sacks, or dig up the oldest rags they can find. I think Christian kids ought to dress attractively and in style. They ought to fit into their world and enjoy looking nice.

But sometimes clothes mean more to a person than looking nice.

Teens in ten high schools were asked not long ago what it took to get into the leading crowd at school. Here's what they said it took for girls:

Wear just the right things, nice hair, good grooming and have a wholesome personality.

Money, clothes, flashy appearance, date older boys, fairly good grades.

Be a sex-fiend—dress real sharp—have own car and money—smoke and drink—go steady with a popular boy.

Have pleasant personality, good manners, dress nicely, be clean, don't swear, be loads of fun.

A nice personality, dress nice without overdoing it.[3]

Notice the common denominator? The kids might disagree on decency, but one thing everyone mentioned was "dress nicely." Clothes. This raises an important question. How much does a person depend on clothes for acceptance? How much of his desire to dress well stems, deep down, from the feeling that worth and acceptance really do depend on how he dresses? "Clothes make the man," they say. So maybe the feeling grows that you've got to have new clothes. You've got to have the latest style. You've got to dress well to feel confident, likable, worthwhile.

When a person feels *that* way about clothes, he's a plain, old-fashioned materialist. He really does depend on things as essential to his real life.

Just last year my older son had told the guys in his junior class that he was going to get some boots just like the ones they had. I said otherwise. He had some good but ugly boots, and we just didn't have the money to invest in new ones. Was he upset! For a while there he was convinced he wasn't going back to school at all! Ever.

So we talked about it. I suggested that boots wouldn't make any difference to his friends. They'd still like him, and he'd still be part of the gang. It was *him* they liked, not his boots. I wasn't very convincing. Still, the next day he went back to school—in the old boots. And we never heard another word about it, except to note that he and Bob and Eddie were just as good buddies as ever.

Having or not having boots really didn't change *him*. His life, his personality, everything that was truly important about him as a person, did not depend on what he possessed. Our real life never does.

But it's a hard lesson to learn for all of us. In our culture many (if not most!) adults haven't learned it. Lots of moms and dads take extra jobs that take them away from their families so they can buy *things* to give them. Which would you rather have? Parents who are available and interested in *you*—or folks who are off earning extra money for a color TV, a larger house, or more and better clothes? Parents who thought and acted as if *you* are important, or as if the things they buy you are important?

So it really is important to learn not to depend on material possessions. We can't build a happy or meaningful life on things. Real life doesn't depend on them. As the Bible says, "We brought absolutely nothing with us when we entered this world and we can be sure we shall take absolutely nothing with us when we leave it. Surely then, as far as physical things are concerned, it is sufficient for us to keep our bodies fed and clothed. For men who set their hearts on being wealthy expose themselves to temptation. They fall into one of the world's traps, and lay themselves open to all sorts of silly and wicked desires, which are quite capable of utterly ruining and destroying their souls" (1 Tim. 6:7-9).

. Things just aren't dependable. No wonder you can't build your life on them.

Trapped?

Materialism may be one of the world's traps; but even if you're in it, don't give up. We always have *choice*. "When I was given a Christmas gift of quite a bit of money," says a girl from Massachusetts, "I had the choice of buying stocks, clothes, or anything. By buying stocks I could make more money and save for the future. By buying clothes I could feel properly outfitted (and gorgeous) for some time. However, I felt this was not right—I had to decide whether to give it away or keep it. It boiled down to what was I living for—me or God? I ended up giving quite a bit away and investing some so it would be making money for future gifts or needs. It's hard to decide in what you really put your trust—God or money."

You probably won't have a big chunk of money dropped in your lap. But you, and I, have to make the same decision she did, and there are ways to tell just where we are now. Here are just a few:

List your most treasured possession(s). Ask yourself, *Why* do I treasure this? Why is it so important to me? Would I feel like myself without it? Do I count on it to gain me acceptance from others? For my sense of security?

When your life seems to depend on things, watch it. You're in the trap, and materialistic values have too strong a control.

Look at your allowance and earnings. How do you use your money? What do you spend it on? *Why* do you spend it that way? What other ways might you use your money?

If you can reason back from the way you use your money to the "What's important to me?" implied, this little exercise will be revealing indeed.

Look at your feelings. This is revealing too. Do you feel frustrated when you don't get something you want? Does it make you depressed? Or, on the other hand, do you feel you could lick the world when you put on a new dress or a new jacket? Do you gain confidence from driving around in your car?

When your self-confidence is jerked around by things, and your sense of security rests in what you own, it's safe to say that things have more power over you than they should—more than you really want them to have!

Somehow people living a real life don't have to draw strength from things. They're strong inside and don't have to trust in their possessions. They've got the kind of trust in God that frees them from being that kind of an emotional cripple.

Steps to take

1. The author suggests that your real values may be hidden from you. How can you discover what your hidden values are?

2. Among hidden values that are common today are materialistic ones. Check yourself out on the amount of control materialistic values may have over you by using the three tests suggested in the final section of the chapter.

3. The Bible says a lot about materialism as a way of life. Check out these three passages from Jesus' own teaching, and see what they add to the present discussion: Luke 12:13-24; Matthew 6:19-34; Matthew 19:16-29.

3

Private property

"How much value should be put on what grown-ups advise or urge us to do?" wonders a California girl. "This is not only applied to Christian things but, well, let me give an example. Since I attend a small school, the boys involved in sports, Student Council, etc., are involved in an awful lot. Some of them were complaining because sometimes they feel pressured into joining a sport like track because of the few guys in our school. The pressure comes from the coaches, and the guys know they shouldn't, because their grades may suffer. Should they just say, 'No, thanks!' and let it be, or should they join and do their best in the sport?"

Everyone has questions like this sometimes. How much of our life is to be lived to please somebody else? Are other's values always to be accepted?

When a young person begins to feel that someone is trying to run his life for him, the offender is usually a parent. The values we're most familiar with are those we've learned from our parents. The point of view we've heard expressed all our lives is theirs.

But when we get out into campus life, we discover other points of view. Sometimes we want to try them out. We begin to question the things we've taken for granted because our parents taught us that way. With the development of "our own ideas," we may come into conflict with mom and dad. No wonder some of the strongest feelings that a person's life is "private property" well up when we differ with them about decisions we want to make for ourselves.

Not everyone who goes through high school and on to a job or to college experiences value conflict. In a way, it's too bad. Why?

"My decisions in high school were never made according to fun or popularity, but always depended on what my parents wanted. Consequently, when I left them behind in college, I couldn't ever decide anything, and still have that trouble." If you get used to letting parents make all your decisions, you'll really be adrift when you finally cut loose from home!

Maybe that's why so many kids who wrote to me spoke up strongly on this issue, and made a big pitch for freedom of choice. "Make your values your own, not your family's," advised a twenty-one-year-old from Texas. "Too often high schoolers just do what's expected of them for no reason of their own."

"A kid has to have his own values," says a girl from overseas, "not just the ones handed down to him by his parents. He has to make up his own mind—even though this is hard to do alone."

This is something everyone has to learn to do—to make up his own mind. It can be tough, particularly because when we look at our pattern of life, and try to reason back to the values behind what we do, we may be fooled. Our relationships with other people—our parents, our friends —may release motivating forces that counterfeit other values. We may think we have our own values and act on them, and be completely fooled!

Bound—and rebound

When a person loves and respects his parents, it's particularly hard to feel a need to develop personal values.

Not that feeling close to mom and dad is bad. In fact, we need their guidance. It's comforting to know that they're there to keep us from making any real bad mistakes, to say "Stop!" when they feel that we're losing control.

But the further a person moves into the teen years, the less helpful it is to "use" parents as a substitute for personal convictions.

"Whenever I am doing something that is really bad that

I shouldn't be doing," says a fifteen-year-old girl, "I always think of my mother and what she would say. I'm always afraid that I would disappoint her if she found out. My friends think I'm terrible because I'll leave or I won't go in with them. But usually afterwards I'm glad that I didn't go along with them."

As I said, this is all right—to a point. But the day is coming when that mental image of mom won't appear. Then, unless we have an anchor in personal values that we've thought through and committed ourselves to, we may be in trouble. As an older girl wrote, "It takes the formation of *our own* individual values outside of public opinion (be that parental, peer group, church, or whatever)."

Why can't we just take over our parents' values wholesale? We can, and maybe we will. Most of us accept a lot of their values, and will all of our lives. Usually our parents' values make a pretty good starting place! But there's a *danger that we'll confuse our "desire to please our parents" with "belief in their values."*

What I mean is this: A guy may *think* that his reason for signing up to be a camp counselor is "spiritual dedication." But his real motive may be the approval of his pastor father. So he signs up because this is what he thinks his father wants.

This kind of motive isn't unusual. One twenty-year-old from Illinois looked back and wrote, "I think in high school I had very vague ideas of what it meant to do God's will. Perhaps I was trying to be overly conscientious about doing what was right and not letting anyone think I was unspiritual." See it? She *thought* that a desire to "do God's will" controlled her actions. Now she looks back and realizes that what was really important to her was "not letting anyone think I was unspiritual." The desire to do what others expected was the *controlling* value.

We can think we accept the values of our parents or our church, and all the time be controlled by our concern to live up to others' expectations. That's a lesson that Bev learned, the hard way. "Being brought up in a strict parsonage, I did have my values. It didn't strike me that these values were not really mine in entirety until they were greatly challenged by a tall, dark, handsome Norwegian. I went with him for a year and, according to some definitions, "fell in love" with him. Then, the validity and reality of those values were really tested, for he was not a Christian, though he was an honest seeker and thinker.

"I rebelled inwardly, although outwardly I still appeared the same. It began to wear me out eventually. I had not the courage to go against what I had been taught and that which I really believed in basically, but I was greatly tempted. And, one by one, "my" values broke down and so did I, emotionally and physically and mentally."

Through the conflict Bev became stronger, so her story really does have a "happy ending." Bev did develop a strong set of *personal* values. But it was no fun, being bound to live by her need to please her folks, and her need to please her boyfriend.

Of course, the rebound is just as bad. What's "rebound"?

Well, being bound is having your parents' approval seem so important to you that you do what they think is right—without ever really developing values of your own. It's *thinking* that you act as you do because something is "God's will" or "the right thing to do," when all along what motivates you is a need to please mom and dad. Rebound is doing the opposite of their values.

Nearly all teenagers have a time of rebound. "As a fifteen-year-old," one guy recalls, "I went through quite a period of rebellion, though it was not observable to most people. In my mind, I questioned the authority of anyone or anything who tried to tell me what to do. I wanted to be my own independent self, and make my own decisions. I believed I was completely capable and did not need to be under anyone's authority, especially adult. I wanted to be treated on an equal level with adults."

That's when rebound comes—when we get the feeling that it's time to make our own decisions, to be free.

Essentially, the desire to be our own self is healthy. It's something that ought to come to each of us in the process of moving toward maturity. No one is mature who wants to be a mama's boy! But the urge to be independent can also deceive. In reacting against the authority of parents, a person can fool himself about his values.

It works like this: Suppose mom and dad are persuaded no Christian ought, ever, to go to a movie. So right now you're on the rebound, feeling a need for independence. What can you do to show you're living on your own now? Well, why not *go* to a movie? After all, you can think of lots of reasons why a good movie (rated "G" yet!) is all-right entertainment. Better than lots of stuff your parents watch on TV! That's it! Now you've thought it through. Now you've got a value of your own to act on. "Good movies are OK." And off you go.

There's only one problem. You may just be *reacting against your parents' values!*

A Texas girl sees rebound this way: "I think many choices made by high schoolers are made by reacting positively or negatively to their parents. One thing that ought to be emphasized is that the teenager should think for himself, but that this doesn't mean react against something. It means evaluate as objectively as you can for yourself."

What it boils down to is this: When a guy or girl thinks about his values, he can be fooled by one of two reactions to his parents: (1) He may be so dependent on mom and dad that he thinks *their* values are his own when all the time what controls his conduct is "Will this please mom and dad?" (2) Or he may be struggling for independence and, as a result, go against his parents' values. What controls his life then is "Will this prove I'm free of adult authority?" It won't be his convictions about the things he chooses to do.

So it's tough. One who is under twenty-one has a hard time looking at the pattern of his life and trying to trace his actions back to the values that lie behind them. Some of the most powerful motives that control him may be hidden.

And the desire to please (or show independence of) parents isn't the only social motive that may power his life. Maybe it's not even the strongest!

Fair exchange

Pick up any studies of adolescence and you'll discover chapters and chapters devoted to the importance of the peer group—the impact that teenagers have on each other. You'll read things like this:

> The family—important as it is as a defining and limiting agency, and as much as it is the central focus of any child's existence—nevertheless cannot usually transcend, nor, indeed, in many cases even meet, the achievement of the peer group in shaping values and in providing perceived personal security as an individual.
> Thus we may see the peer world, for most adolescents, as a tremendously important source of attitudes, the inhibitor as well as the initiator of action, the arbiter of right and wrong.[1]

This is a rather long-winded way of saying just what Danny felt when he went into junior high:

"During my first couple of years in junior high school the pressure from the gang to attain low grades was unbelievable. Kids wouldn't tell anybody about getting good grades, but I almost bragged about pulling a 'D' on a test. In fact, I did. I got this social pressure from my peers to keep the class curve down, but at the same time my folks and counselors advised me to get good grades so that I would do good in high school and college."

In place of pressures to act to please his parents, Danny felt pressures to please the other kids. *He exchanged parents' control of his decisions for control by his friends!*

This is an exchange that almost all of us make in some areas of life. For instance, what teen doesn't realize that the kids at school know a lot more about clothes and hair style than his parents? What the kids think here seems a lot more sensible.

But often a guy or girl will hand over control of far more important decisions to friends.

Now, friends are awfully important to someone in his teens or early twenties. And that's all right. During these years friends ought to be important. It's by associating with fellows and girls their same age that older young people grow socially and learn how to get along with people outside their family. But at times these friends may become too important.

One study of Lutheran young people showed that other kids were so important that "goals that might be classified as social values" ranked near the top of what the kids said was "important to me." "Being a person well liked by everyone" was the top value, and "enjoying good times with others" came in number four on a list of forty items.[2]

Again, this isn't necessarily bad. The influence of the

group, as the influence of parents, can be good. That influence can help us discover some of the most important values in life. A Montana guy tells how being in a Christian group helped him take steps that he'd never have been able to take alone. "I remember the first time I ran into a group who had a plan for something I had wanted to do but didn't really know how. That was witnessing. One evangelistic organization had a plan and someone to teach various collegians how to communicate the Gospel now. This said to me, 'You can do what Christ commanded if you want to. We've tried this, and it works for us.' Here then was a disturbing decision, for how could I fool myself into thinking I was a Christian and turn down an opportunity that had bothered me for a long time?" So he joined the group—and made it.

Actually, our relationship with the gang can have the same impact on our lives that family relationships can. It motivates us to do helpful things—or harmful ones. The influence of friends may seem "bad" (motivating us to get low grades to keep the curve down) or "good" (encouraging us and helping us to get out and witness). But, good or bad, the thing to remember is that the pressures to "fit in" can tell us about our values. We may do something and think, *That's the way I really feel about it* when, in fact, we're not thinking and feeling for ourselves at all. The "What's important to me?" behind our actions may be concerned for what the other kids will think.

Now, I hope I've made myself clear on this. I don't object to having what others think about us matter. I think it should. I believe we should care about parents and their approval. I believe we should care about our friends, and want to fit into their world. I hope you care too. But in the struggle to develop your own values and live by your own convictions, you ought to be aware of the power others may have over you. You ought to check to make sure that what you're doing isn't really controlled by someone else.

Personally, I don't think we should care *so much* that what others will think of us becomes the only value we apply in making our choices. That's not acting responsibly. You see, a person's life is *his*. Not mom's or dad's. Not the gang's. His. Someday he's going to give account of it, and he's the one who will be held responsible for what he does.

Actually, I want to check my values out against the values of others. I want to know why my parents and my friends think and feel and act as they do. Living with others, I can discover how some of their values work out in practice, how the values affect their lives. But seeing others' values and drawing some of my own values from them (which everyone does) is not the same as depending on their approval. It's not the same as living life *their way*.

And that's what we have to watch out for—being fooled—thinking that we have the same values as the people we care about, when we're controlled not by values but by a desire to win their approval.

That kind of sick dependence on others fools a lot of people, and we all need to watch out for it.

Check points

"I'll always remember a decision I made in my senior year in high school," says a twenty-one-year-old college girl. "It was about the prom. I was asked all four years in high school, but had always refused because I knew my mom wouldn't like it, and I figured I'd go my senior year. Senior year came, and all of a sudden I was faced with *my own decision*."

She'd discovered what it means to insist on your life

being private property. It's just what it means for you—
that all your life you'll be faced with your own decisions.

Before we can dig into what this means and see how to
test and choose our own values, it's important to check a
few points and see where you stand now. Make sure the
opinions of others aren't crowding out all other values,
cutting you out of chances to learn by making decisions
on your own. How can a guy or girl tell? Here are some
possible clues to look for:

Check "close correspondence." Do your views *always*
match mom and dad's? Do you find it hard to see the other
side of any question they feel strongly about? Then you
may be "bound," not responding to their values, but
looking for their approval.

On the other hand, if your views and ideas differ mark-
edly from theirs, you may be on the rebound. You may
not decide things on the basis of values you hold, but on
whether you feel a need to prove you're grownup and
independent. Either way you can be fooled into thinking
you hold values that aren't really your own.

Check the intensity of your feelings. In differences between your parents' values and those of the gang, do you
feel an *intense* loyalty to one or the other? Do your feelings
swell up and overwhelm you so that you've just got to
stick up for one point of view—no matter what it is? It's
likely then that your real concern is for someone's approval. Not that you can't feel strongly about values themselves. But if the slightest criticism throws your feelings
into high, it's a danger sign.

Check the viewpoint from which you evaluate. A Christian
is extremely concerned about one Person's approval:
God's. Are the values you're acting on in harmony with
His? "As children copy their fathers, you, as God's children, are to copy him" the Bible says (Eph. 5:1). That kind

of copying requires that we know what God's values are, and what in human experience is important to Him.

Being a Christian gives a person an *objective* way to evaluate his feelings and his decisions too. This really helps. It means that we don't have to live, tossed from one person's way of looking at life to another's, with no assurance of whose way is right. It means that we can take that "private property" life of ours and know what we're doing when we commit it.

I hope you'll want to know what you're doing with your life, and why.

Being a puppet, tugged around all your life by mom and dad or by the gang, or even by the church, is a pretty poor substitute for really living.

Life is meant to have a lot more meaning than *that*. For you.

Steps to take

1. Look over the list of "What's important to me?" you made after reading chapter 1. On the basis of what's been said in this chapter, how would you relate them to what your parents and your friends believe and do?

2. Check through the "danger signals" at the end of this chapter, and use them to look at yourself.

3. Think about it. What do you do just because your friends approve of it? What do you do just because your parents approve of it? What do you do just because *you* approve of it?

4

On impulse

Have you ever worked hard to think up reasons for doing something you wanted to do? And then tried to convince yourself that it was because of the reasons that you felt the desire all along?

You have? Then welcome to the club. So has everyone else.

Feelings hit us from all directions. Some are strong and long-lasting. One son of a missionary at school in the Philippines wanted desperately to go back home and take his schooling by correspondence. "I was in a boarding school away from my parents, and I wanted to leave because of a lot of unhappy relationships."

A sixteen-year-old felt generally rebellious and mixed up: "As a freshman I was very rebellious both toward my parents and Christian things. I was (and am) very active in the young people's group and was in all athletics and many other school functions. I really don't understand what got into me. I must have been a little devil! Then I got involved with this boy who was probably the rottenest boy around. Sure, he was good-looking, athletic, and had anything else a girl would want. My parents tried to break us up after they realized how messed up our relationship was, and how bitter I was getting. It didn't work." Feelings like this can grab control of a person's life—and hold on.

There are other kinds of feelings too—feelings that well up in an instant, and cause us to act on impulse.

—You look at the books and then at a football. "Oh well, I'll just toss it around for a while."

—The gang is standing around after school, with nothing to do. "Let's take a ride," somebody says. Why not? So off you go.

—You're walking by a magazine counter, and there's a bunch of those girlie magazines hitting you right in the eye. You glance around, pick one up, and look to see what's on the center fold.

—"Hey, you oughta try one of these," says a guy, holding out a little green pill. "It's wild!" You pick it up. Just once won't hurt. And you pop it in your mouth to see what it's like.

—You're at home, and your kid sister has left some of her stuff on your desk. You mutter, "Darn her anyway," and knock it off on the floor.

—It's the night before a big test. You sit there looking at the words, and your hand reaches out to turn on the radio. Soon you're beating time with the newest song from your favorite group.

—*Someday I'm gonna pick up this room*, you think, and kick a shoe under the bed.

—You're parked outside her house, out in back. It's late, and you've been making out for half an hour. You think, *I wonder what it would be like?* And you—

—"Don't forget those cases of vegetables," the boss

says. That did it! Burning, you jerk off your apron, toss it on the floor, and walk out.

That's life

"I want" and "I have an impulse to—" are always part of our human experience. Just being people means that

we're going to *feel*. And this is a good thing. Why? Well, listen to the story of this guy from Kentucky: "The majority of my decisions in high school were based on my sense of duty and of responsibility. Because of this, almost any job that came along I accepted. I became so involved that I lost contact with God and with all my friends."

That sounds like a pretty grim life to me. Never doing things because they're fun, or because you want to. Always doing things because you feel it's your duty, or "a responsibility." Living this way, a person loses out on a lot of experiences that should be a part of life.

So when we think about "I want to" and "I feel like it" as motives for actions, it would be wrong to classify them as "bad."

It's a lot like the things we've thought about in the last two chapters. Are material things sinful? Not in themselves. What's right or wrong, helpful or harmful, is our response to them. The Bible says that God gave us all things in this world "richly to enjoy." But when material things become so important to us that our choices are controlled by them, then *we're* wrong. Our values are way out of balance.

It's not sinful to be concerned about others' approval. But when gaining approval becomes the controlling motive in our life, something is wrong—with us.

It's like this with our desires and impulses. Is it wrong to *feel?* No. In fact, we'd be wrong to try to live apart from emotion. We'd be wrong to push all our desires aside as "sinful." When Jesus was on earth, He didn't do that. He enjoyed a wedding party. He liked being in the company of His friends. He was deeply moved at the sight of suffering. He got angry when people, like the Pharisees, showed themselves hardhearted and unconcerned. He lived the life of a *whole* person, with a full range of human emotions and desires just like ours. In fact, the Bible tells us that the night before He was crucified He *felt* the situation so deeply that He cried out in agony to God.

So don't get the weird idea that a person shouldn't feel pressure and want out of tough experiences, or shouldn't feel relaxed and enjoy good times. In fact, it's not wrong even to feel a momentary desire for *wrong* things! No, the problem with feelings is that sometimes we may throw up our hands and turn control of our life over to them. That's what happened to Arlene.

"I was dating a guy my senior year in high school whom I didn't really like. Our relationship was a purely physical one. Everyone knew what kind of guy he was, and my friends started looking down on me for going with him. They had expected better things from me, told me I could do a lot better, etc. But I didn't do anything about it. I didn't at the time want to give up the 'sex.'

"But I kept remembering a paper I had written for home ec. class, entitled "My Top-10 Values.' Tops on my list I had written that I wanted a happy marriage and family, based on Christian love and Christian principles. This guy and I had a long talk one day. I had mentioned a few times before that I thought it would be better not to see each other anymore. But this time I told him about this list of values I had written, saying that if we kept on as we were I certainly wouldn't be living up to them. I was surprised that he realized the importance of this and encouraged me to do what I thought best. Well, I hung on for a while, all the time wondering what would become of me, as I would be enrolling in college the next month. Finally I decided these values were more important to me than any immediate gratification.

"I'm sorry now that it ever happened, but I'm glad I stopped it before I had something to be really sorry for. I put a lot more weight now on my values, and more thought to my future than to my present desires."

See what she's saying? Feelings, emotions, impulses —part of life though they are—are all *now* kinds of things. They push us to respond immediately. But feelings don't evaluate. They can't guarantee what we'll feel after we have acted on them. They can't tell us the results of the actions they motivate.

We have to stand as judge over our feelings.

We've all had to face this kind of thing—the balancing of present desires against other values. Some of us have to balance the desire to have another piece of chocolate cake against what that will do to our waistline. We even have to decide whether to give in to feelings when we get up tight, or not. "A bit ago," says a fifteen-year-old, "I was put on extra study hours because of low grades. Usually I immediately start griping about something like this, but I decided to take that age-old advice and look on the brighter side. I made up my mind not to get mad about it, and soon I saw that if I did study longer my grades would go up, so I really did need the extra time. I found that I was much happier with an attitude like this."

Strong feelings and urges *demand* in all of us. But each of us knows that he can master them. We can decide which desires to satisfy, and which to put off. We do it all the time.

So feelings, such an essential part of our experience, aren't wrong in themselves. They aren't a problem unless we hand our life over to them and say, "You take control!"

Much happier

A study of Christian teenagers that I mentioned earlier shows that "happiness is the life goal for most of the youth [*surveyed*], whereas personal achievement and service commanded the interest of a minority."[1] The researcher goes on to say that this "well-nigh universal" valuing of happiness "seems to describe a natural yearning after 'godliness with contentment,' though the primary hue seems basically hedonistic."[2]

That word *hedonistic* is often used to describe older high schoolers and collegians. But as a matter of fact, the idea that happiness is *pleasurable experience now* is the older generation's idea too! William Kvaraceus points out that "American living has been moving rapidly from a work-oriented to a play-oriented culture." He says, "If the delinquent is sometimes viewed as pleasure-bent, riding heavily on a want-it-now track, it is because he is surrounded by elders who set the pattern. . . . The adult lesson of self-indulgence is not lost on youth."[3]

It's true. Pretty often the "American way" is to indulge ourselves and our desires just as much as we can!

That leads to the idea that the way to achieve happiness is to find and enjoy pleasure experiences—of anything.

How does this view of life stack up? Is this giving free rein to our feelings and desires the way to happiness?

There are lots of reasons to hesitate before buying this view. One reason is that we know from experience it doesn't work. Doing what you want to do does not automatically lead to happiness, and sometimes doing what you *don't* want to do does!

Jay wanted to be a basketball star and thought that he had it all locked up. "At the beginning of my senior year, I was sure of a position on the starting five of our varsity basketball team. Our church group planned a retreat for a weekend fairly early in the season. In order to go I would have to miss a special Saturday practice. I asked permission from my coach, and he exploded. He said that if I went, I'd sit on the bench for the rest of the season.

"I went. And I lost my starting position. But at the retreat I decided to go to a certain Bible school. There my life was dedicated to God, and the attitudes I learned and the friends I met have changed my life. This, to date, is the biggest decision I have had to make. It was a decision between what I literally lived for—basketball, and what I was dedicated to—God. I chose for God, and I'm glad I did." Maybe you've had desires or impulses that you've overruled too—and later been glad about it.

Sure, pleasurable experiences are pleasurable. Doing what we want to do when we want to do it may look like a great way of life. But there's no guarantee that this leads to happiness, or that happiness and pleasure feelings are the same thing! Actually, most Christians don't quite trust their desires—with good reason. We've all *wanted* to do something our conscience told us was wrong. And we've all done wrong things that we wanted to, and felt guilty afterward!

There's another reason why we feel that it's dangerous to trust our desires and impulses completely: the dozens of warnings against this kind of thing in the Bible. These are warnings about becoming "slaves of various desires and pleasant feelings" (Titus 3:3), and against letting our "character be molded by the desires of your ignorant days" (1 Peter 1:14). In fact, the Bible says we Christians have "no particular reason to feel grateful to our sensual nature, or to live life on the level of the instincts. Indeed that way of living leads to certain spiritual death. But if on the other hand you cut the nerve of your instinctive actions by obeying the Spirit, you are on the way to real living" (Rom. 8:12-13).

While we can accept ourselves as feeling, emotional beings, we are not to be *ruled* by our instincts.

The Bible doesn't say this to cut us out of happiness but to lead us to happiness. God tells us that from birth our emotional and instinctive equipment has been faulty. Even as a radio that's been jarred in a plane crash transmits and receives distorted signals, our equipment may be so damaged that we're having a hard time telling what the vibrations really mean. This is the heart of what the Bible means when it says that we're "sinners." All our equipment—feelings, mind, will—has been so smashed by sin that we can't trust it. We can't trust it to lead us to happiness, and we certainly can't trust it enough to turn our life over to our desires and say, "You run things. I'll just sit back and enjoy the ride!" Our experience bears this out. Running on desires and impulses just isn't safe.

Remember Arlene, who let her desire for "immediate gratification" control her relationship with her boyfriend? Look over her experience again (p. 45). What do you think this did to her self-respect? What feelings do you think lie behind the words "Well, I hung on for a while, all the time wondering what would become of me"? Did letting this desire take charge lead her to happiness? No. And according to the Bible, turning life over to our desires leads mankind and individuals to "inevitable disintegration" (2 Peter 1:4).

Cart, or horse?

There is something we ought to settle about our relationship with our desires and impulses. Who pulls whom? Do they govern and pull us around, dictating our choices? Or will *we* make the choices and have our feelings fall in line with them?

You can have it either way.

That's an important principle to get straight. If a person turns control over to his feelings and does what they dictate, he will become the slave of "various desires and pleasant feelings" that the Bible talks about. But if he asserts his control over his life, considering his feelings but deciding firmly with reference to other values as well, he'll find that his feelings *change!*

When one is in front, the other will follow—sooner or later.

Arlene decided to stop something that she *liked* because of her values. For a while she didn't want to "give it up." But then she did, and now her feelings have changed radically. "I'm sorry now that it ever happened," she says, and "glad I stopped it."

Feelings can change and *do* change. That's another reason they don't make a good guide to decisions. And when you begin to live by other values, your feelings will tag along behind.

This leaves us about where we started back on page one—with a need for other values to live by. "I think," says a seventeen-year-old from Minnesota, "that a book such as this should be realistic. A lot of people make decisions for unknown reasons. I think a Christian should make them on a different level, but a lot of us don't. There are always other influences."

It's those "other influences" that we've talked about so far—those "unknown reasons" that control so many of us. Each is another vital reason why we need clear-cut values: So we won't unknowingly turn our life over to empty materialism. So we won't turn ourselves over to others—to dangle meaninglessly through life as they pull the strings. So we won't just follow our impulses and desires—to be pushed and pulled by "pleasurable feelings" that destroy our character in return for momentary satisfactions.

Yet, to take control we need values to steer by.

Choosing them is important.

It's really choosing the kind of person you'll become.

Steps to take

1. Evaluate these two statements:

   a. The best way of being sure you do the right thing is to do just the opposite of what you want to do!

   b. A guy is a fool not to do what he wants whenever he can. After all, we only live once, so we'd better enjoy ourselves now!

2. The author spoke a lot about happiness in this chapter, but he didn't try to define it. What do *you* think happiness is? How does a good dictionary define it?

3. Check out the pattern of your own daily life. How many things do you do or refuse to do just because you "want to"?

   Do you think that your feelings are grabbing control away from you, or do you have control over them?

4. Look over the list of "What's important to me?" you made earlier. Would you change it now? How?

5

Why all the fuss?

"In high school I had very little trouble making decisions," writes a Pennsylvania girl. "I knew what I wanted, and I went after it in any honest method possible. Only since I've learned that there are more philosophies in the world than I ever dreamed of, have value conflicts arisen in my decision-making."

The more you think about *why* you act as you do, the more complicated it all seems. The more you try to decide what your values are, the hazier the whole idea of values and decisions seems to become.

Before we can get very far in choosing our own values and in learning to live by them, we need to know more about what values are, and how they work in daily life.

I was interested to see that some of the guys and girls who helped with this book mixed up *values* with things like smoking, dancing and drinking.

"I guess the most difficult thing I did," says a boy from Vermont, "was to stop dancing. However, I'd like to make it *very* clear that there was actually no pressure at all from home (my parents were not Christians) nor from the church (many of the teens danced). I guess I just decided it was the 'right thing to do,' and I really didn't miss it nearly as much as I thought I would."

On the other hand, a sixteen-year-old from North Carolina writes, "Even though raised in a Christian home, such decisions concerning drinking, smoking, petting and dancing don't always come easy. However, because my parents brought me up the way they did, and because I belong to God, I can *not* do these things because it's not right for me and not what God wants for me."

While several shared their thoughts about this kind of decision, others reacted strongly to all the rules and lists of dos and don'ts they've run into. "If you want to focus on values, focus on the right ones," says a college girl. "Today far too much emphasis is placed on some of the social norms by churches and Christian parents while the real issues and answers kids are searching for are somewhere in the nebulous."

A Connecticut girl says, "Let's not talk about the negative, binding, no-reason-for-why-not 'no's' that Christian kids get too hung up on, and whether dancing, smoking, and drinking are correct behavior. Christianity has been placing too much emphasis on the external values. How about placing it on Christ's values?"

Now, I don't know which side you're on. You may want to "hold the line," feeling that don'ts are important assets to Christian witness, and a part of our separation from the world. You may be on the "freedom" side that insists such things are irrelevant, and that we ought to think more about loving and showing love. But if we want to get down to values, we'd all better realize that this particular issue has nothing to do with them!

That's right. The dos and don'ts are *not* (repeat, *not!*)

values. And they should never be confused with values. At best, the lists are derived from values, or reflect values. But they are not values themselves.

Figure 1
Decisions can be traced back to values

Decision	Reason given for making it	Value area indicated by reason
not to smoke	it's wrong	right/wrong
	tried it, didn't like it	personal pleasure
	boys don't like to see a girl smoke	what the boys think
	most think it's not good for you	view of majority
	stains teeth, fingers; smells up hair, clothing, car	personal attractiveness
	bad for health	health
	friends all agree, a matter for individual choice	what friends think

This is pretty easy to demonstrate. Take this decision reported by Jan, an Illinois girl: "I faced a decision of whether to smoke or not, and there were several reasons why I decided not to. I believed smoking was wrong. I tried it and didn't really like it. Most people think it's not good for you, and boys have told me they don't like to see a girl smoke. It's bad for your health, stains your teeth and fingers, and makes your hair, clothes, car and house smell horrible. I felt no pressure to smoke or look cool or anything. My friends and I all agree that it's up to the individual, and we don't try to force anybody to do something they don't want to."

Now, wouldn't it be foolish to say of Jan, "One of her values is not smoking"?

The values that affected her decision are reflected in the reasons she gives for it. And even here it's impossible to tell what is really "important to her"—so important that it would have a controlling impact on what she does and doesn't do. Just look at all the different values that had some impact on Jan's decision (Fig. 1).

Jan's experience does more for us than indicate that values are a behind-the-scenes type of thing. It shows us something important about how values function in our experience and how they affect our decision-making.

I suppose the simplest way to say what happens is that *we see what we're looking for.*

What we're looking for

Put in big words, values provide a perceptual grid which gives a selective orientation to situations. Taken out of big words, it's a lot easier to understand.

Let's say that five people are standing on a street corner, watching a smiling girl stride up the sidewalk. One is a dentist, one a hairdresser, one a dressmaker, one a coach, and one an optometrist. What does each see? Well, the dentist notices first her smile and white, even teeth. The hairdresser notices the way her hair is cut and shaped, and if it fits her type of face. The first thing the dressmaker sees is the way her outfit is cut and trimmed. The coach notes her athletic swing, and the way she carries her head and shoulders. And the optometrist, noting a slight squint, wonders if she has glasses and doesn't wear them because she thinks they might spoil her looks!

This is an example of a "perceptual grid" that "gives a selective orientation" to situations. That is, the interests and past experiences of each of the five made him look at the girl differently than the others. Each looked for different things, and each saw what he was looking for! While all may have been vaguely aware of the features that drew the attention of the others, it's possible—even likely— that *only* the optometrist noted the girl's slight squint.

Why did it work this way? Because, to each, one feature was more important to him (the perceptual grid) than other features. He naturally looked first of all at (selected) that which was most important to him!

We operate this way all the time. Let's say you're going to a party at a friend's house. You go in and glance around the room. What grabs your attention? Maybe you see a lot of kids you don't know, and look quickly for some friends. Maybe your attention is drawn to some oil paintings on the wall. Maybe you hear music coming

from the patio, and immediately head out there. Maybe
you head over to the snack table in one corner of the
room, and grab a plateful. Or maybe you go to the rest
room to check your makeup and hairdo.

Now, coming into that room, all these sights and
sounds hit you at once—the music, the kids standing
around talking, the pictures on the wall, the snacks piled
on the table—everything. But you focused on *one*. Your
perceptual grid unconsciously filtered out the things that
didn't particularly interest you—the sights and sounds
that didn't "click" with something inside you—and
selected something you *were* interested in. In other
words, you saw what you were looking for—and probably weren't even aware of the process!

Our *values* operate the same way in decision-making
that our interests do at a party. Our values filter out the
factors that don't seem important to us, and focus our
attention on what *is* important to us. And we tend to base
our decisions on the factors that we see.

For instance, think back over the reasons Jan gave for
not smoking. I said earlier they give us a clue to her
values. They point out, by the very fact that she selected
them for consideration, what is really most important to
her. What seem to be some of her values? Well, whether
or not she *likes* something. What the boys think. What her
friends think. How something affects her appearance and
her health, and so on. But, did you notice the factors she
did *not* seem to consider? Like, What will my parents
think? What's the position of the church on this? What
will smoking do to my testimony? Now, maybe her parents and her church don't care about smoking, and in her
society Christians smoke if they want to. Whatever the
reason, in this particular situation some things were important to her, and others (which to someone else might

have seemed crucial) simply were not! She just never thought of them.

Our values, then, have a great impact on what factors we consider when we make decisions. What is important to us is what we're likely to see, and what isn't important we may not even think of.

And if our values are the wrong ones?

Then we go through life seeing it out of focus.

We face decisions, and may not even be aware of key factors we ought to consider.

We develop a pattern of life that leads us further and further away from what real life is intended to be.

So we need *right* values—values that will let us see life as it really is, and live it in a truly meaningful way.

Right and wrong values?

As one psychologist puts it, "Values refer to what we regard as important, rather than to what we know."[1] This, to many people, makes it impossible to talk about values being "right" or "wrong." For instance, I happen to like the color green. My wife likes blue. Am I right about colors, and she wrong? Of course not! Such likes and dislikes can't be right or wrong; they just *are*. On the other hand, if I think that 2 x 2 equals 4, and she thinks that 2 x 2 equals 6, one of us *is* wrong. And we can know it.

So there's a big difference between things that are just personal preferences, and others that have to fit the facts.

That is a big issue when it comes to thinking about values. Are a person's values just a personal preference, or is there some objective measure that makes one set of values right and another set wrong?

Take this statement of humanistic values by Corliss Lamont: "In the Humanist ethics the chief end of thought and action is to further this-earthly human interests on behalf of the greater glory of man. The watch-word of Humanism is happiness for all humanity in this existence."[2] Is this value right or wrong? How can we tell?

Lamont goes on to explain that a person who takes a humanistic view of life sees "the good" as human happiness, and seeks to "weave into a sustained pattern of happiness under the guidance of reason" all the "many sided possibilities for good in human living." In other words, in a decision-making situation the humanist looks first for factors that affect happiness. And "happiness"? Lamont describes it as

> a profound and passionate affirmation of the joys and beauties, the braveries and idealism, of existence on this earth. [Humanism] heartily welcomes all life-enhancing and healthy pleasures, from the vigorous enjoyments of youth to the contemplative delights of mellowed age, from the simple gratifications of food and drink, sunshine and sports, to the more complex appreciation of art and literature, friendship and social communion. Humanism believes in the beauty of love and the love of beauty. It exults in the pure magnificence of external nature.[3]

Boiled down, then, this value system suggests that happiness is experienced of the varied pleasures available in this world. So when decisions are to be made, the humanist prefers to make them on the basis of whether or not a choice seems to diminish or to enhance the chance for such happiness.

Now, there is certainly no question that we are to freely enjoy all the good things God has given us. But the Christian would usually suggest that there is more to life than personal enjoyment, or even than helping others to enjoy this particular brand of happiness. He would look for other factors, and consider several things far more important than happiness.

Why this disagreement about values? Why does one prefer to value human happiness on earth supremely, and the other say that there are things that are more important? Lamont asserts, "Humanism definitely places the destiny of man within the very broad limits of this natural world."[4] It says that this life is all. The destiny of each individual is to live out his span of years on earth, and die, and death is the end. So a man has to find his meaning and his fulfillment in this world.

The Christian believes that each of us has a personal, conscious existence that *never* ends. So the Christian looks for his meaning and fulfillment in the totality of life, not just in life on this earth. It's as the apostle Paul says in talking of the resurrection: "Why should I live a life of such hourly danger? I assure you, by the certainty of Jesus Christ that we possess, that I face death every day of my life! And if, to use the popular expression, I have 'fought with wild beasts' here in Ephesus, what is the good of an ordeal like that if there is no life after this one? Let us rather eat, drink and be merry, for tomorrow we die!" (1 Cor. 15:30-32).

Do you see what he's saying? It's that our idea of "What is important to me?" rests ultimately on our idea of what life is all about, on our idea of what is *real*. That's what the Bible means when it says that human philosophies and values are "at best founded on men's ideas of the nature of the world" (Col. 2:8).

So value preferences aren't like color preferences at all. For our value preference can correspond with (or miss!) reality! If the values we hold don't match up with the way things really are, they are wrong—and we're in trouble! Because our decisions, affected by our values, are going to lead us further and further from really living.

That's what Jesus was saying when He laid down that

principle we looked at earlier: "Guard against covetousness. . . . For a man's real life in no way depends upon
the number of his possessions." A person may value possessions supremely. He may decide to be a "success" in
life and make a million. He may choose a job on the basis
of the financial security it offers, or choose a college course
because of the job opportunities it opens upon graduation. But if he looks for meaning there, or for security,
he'll find neither, because valuing possessions is wrong.
The value doesn't fit the facts.

Real life just doesn't consist of piling up things.

Illusion-busting

Let's try to put all this together. So far we've seen that
values are not the things that we do or don't do, or even
the reasons we find for our actions. Values are our deep
underlying ideas about what is important in life.

Say a friend asks you to "help him out" by saying he
spent last evening with you!

There are a number of reasons you might give for whatever you do. If you say, "Yes, he was with me," some
reasons for this action might be:

1. You gave him your word.
2. You've got to be loyal to friends.
3. His parents are unfair to him anyway.
4. You owe him a favor.
5. It might get him in trouble if you don't.
6. Maybe he'll do the same for you someday.
7. If he tells the gang you let him down, they'll all think
   you're a rat.

On the other hand, if you say, "No, he wasn't with
me," some reasons you might give are:

1. It's wrong for you to lie, even if you promised to in a
   moment of weakness.

2. Parents have their kids' best interests at heart and ought to know what's going on.
3. Telling the truth works out best in the end.
4. You were just waiting for a chance to get back at him!
5. If your folks ever found out you lied for him, they'd kill you.
6. It just isn't the way you have been taught.

Now, which sound like the best reasons to you? Which would convince you? As you can see, there are arguments on both sides. The fact is, your values and your view of what is important in life (or what life is like) will *determine the reasons that seem to you to have the most force!*

So values not only work in our lives to select factors that we think of; they also determine what we think and feel about each factor we consider!

See now why we need to make a fuss about values? Our values, so often unexamined and hidden from us, are crucial in determining the kind of person we become, and the kind of life we choose to lead. So all of us need to ask some serious questions about our values. Questions like What *is* important to me? Are my values the *right* values? Do they harmonize with what life is really all about, or will they lead me into a world of illusion, a never-never land where I'll grope blindly for a real and satisfying way of life, and never find it?

Here Christians have a unique advantage. We can *know* what reality is like, and what life is all about. We can build our values to harmonize with the facts. The unbelievers, the Bible says, "live blindfold in a world of illusion, and are cut off from the life of God through ignorance and insensitiveness" (Eph. 4:18). But the person who shares God's life in Christ and lives close to Him "has an insight into the meaning of everything, though his insight may baffle the man of the world. This is because the former is sharing in God's wisdom, and 'Who hath known the mind of the Lord, That he should instruct him?' Incredible as it may sound, we who are spiritual have the very thoughts of Christ!'' (1 Cor. 2:15-16).

No illusions here. We have a window on reality.

So illusion-busting is one of God's greatest concerns for us. "We are asking God," says Paul in Colossians, "that you may see things, as it were, from his point of view by being given spiritual insight and understanding" (1:9). When we begin to shape up our values, learning to see things from God's point of view and feel about them as He does, our whole life will change.

Steps to take

1. Write out in your own words how values work in your life. Then check over the chapter again to see how well you've understood it.

2. Check over the "What's important to me?" list from chapter 1. If *values* are understood as "our deepest feelings and ideas about what is important in life," rather than our actions or even our reasons for our actions, are what you jotted down really values?

   Now put the list aside, and write out "My Top-Ten Values" as of right now.

3. Look over the reasons given in pages 62 and 63 for a yes or no answer to the mother of our friend. Which reason seemed most significant to you? The author feels that reason number 3 under the "No" list is most significant. Read 3:13–4:1 of 1 Peter and see if you can see what idea about the way things really are makes him feel this way.

6

The "big picture"

A twenty-one-year-old college student says, rather bitterly I think, "Teenagers who limit their perspectives to their little high school world of popularity and brownie-the-teacher and how-much-fun and/or trouble can I get into now, will grow poorly during the high school years. I believe a student can become institutionalized into the high school frame of reference—a small, unreal world, limited to a teenage subculture, just as 'professional students' of years and years of college and grad school become used to the world and routine of the university, competitive scholastic life, an unreal world without true responsibility. This is avoiding life."

Compare what she says, bitter or not, with what Paul says about ignoring the big picture to the Colossians: "Give your heart to the heavenly things, not to the passing things of earth" (3:2).

Ever get the feeling that "spiritual" advice, like the Bible verses quoted in the preceding paragraph, is kind of unreal? It may seem especially unreal when you read the whole context:

If you then are "risen" with Christ, reach out for the highest gifts of Heaven, where Christ reigns in power. Give your heart to the heavenly things, not to the passing things of earth. For, as far as this world is concerned, you are already dead, and your true life is a hidden one in God, through Christ. One day Christ, the secret center of our lives, will show himself openly, and you will all share in that magnificent dénouement (Col. 3:1-4).

I confess that it has seemed pretty unreal to me, too—until I put it in the context of *values*. Then it becomes completely practical. What does it say about values? Something like this.

As a Christian, you ought to see through humanistic

illusions—right through to the reality of heaven and Christ's rule over all things. This insight ought to control your thinking so that human ideas of what is important, which rest on human ideas of what is real, will have no effect on you. As far as such values are concerned, you might as well be dead! But do be alive and responsive to God's view of things, revealed to us through Christ. Don't worry about the fact that this viewpoint is hidden to some of your friends. When Christ comes back, everyone will see things God's way, because He will show Himself to them. Then you'll stand right up there beside Him, and everyone will finally understand why you made the decisions you did and acted as you did.

Far from being unreal and "spiritual," this advice is bluntly practical. And we've seen why. It's practical because our idea of reality, our view of life, shapes the values which determine our way of life.

In fact, the Bible ties our ability to live a Christian life and develop Christian character to an understanding of the big picture—an awareness of what God has planned and what God is doing in human history. "We thank God . . . ," Paul says to the Colossians, "because you are showing true Christian love toward other Christians. We know that you are showing these qualities *because you have grasped the hope reserved for you in Heaven"* (Col. 1:3-5)! Somehow, knowing what God has for us frees us to show real love to others.

A little later we'll try to see *why* understanding the big picture makes such a difference in our lives. But first we'd better ask what the big picture is. It isn't that high school or college society you live in now. It isn't even the society I live in, or our country, or our Western culture. The big picture encompasses all of time, and eternity too!

The Old Testament picture of God's plan

The Old Testament spans in history and prophecy the period from creation to eternity future. Primarily, it tells the story of God's plan for mankind, focused in the experience and the future of a particular people, the Jews.

Insight into God's plan for men begins with a portrait of His building a world for us to live in. Here we were to enjoy His creation and to live in closest friendship with Him. But man wasn't satisfied to live close to God. He wanted to break off from Him and go it alone. The first pair did just this, introducing a strain of driving rebellion in all their children—right down to us.

So the problem God faced was "How are men in rebellion to be brought again into harmony? How are they going to discover what turning away from Me means, not only to Me, but also in the warping of their own character and motivation and behavior?"

It didn't take long for us to find out what *sin*, the biblical word for that rebellious nature of ours, means. One of Adam's sons killed his own brother (Gen. 4), and soon a culture developed in which even murder was rationalized and justified. Men who were out of harmony with God couldn't seem to get along with each other and, before long, all the things we wonder about today—war, disease, suffering, using and hurting others for personal gain—were on the scene.

Genesis 6–8 describes God's great act of judgment; the causing of a tremendous worldwide flood which destroyed a whole race of men, leaving only eight people to start the race over again. They did start over again, but their inner nature had not been changed. Soon the rebellion and selfishness that had ruined the earlier world led to the same conditions on this new world—conditions that haven't changed much right up to now.

In Genesis 12 the Bible shows God taking a different tack. He selects one man, Abraham, and promises to focus His revelation and His purpose in his descendants, the Israelites. After three generations, seventy went down into Egypt. In four hundred years there they were finally enslaved, but they grew to a people of probably two million. Then God sent Moses to lead them out of Egypt back to Palestine, a land He had promised to their father Abraham. On the trip God gave these people a revelation of Himself and His character and a set of laws to live by and the promise that—as they conformed to His purpose for them—He would bless them and care for them.

You know pretty well too that these people were just as rebellious as the rest of us. A few generations stayed pretty close to God, and God did bless them and strengthen their nation. But most of the time the God-like character which His laws portrayed simply was not reproduced in His people. They liked their own way too much.

You know about their ups and downs too. They were defeated in wars and taken out of their land into captivity. Just as Israel is today, they were surrounded by powerful enemies, and lived on the edge of destruction nearly all the time.

Yet, through all this experience, individuals in the nation who trusted God held a particularly strong hope. For God had told them the purpose for which they were called and preserved. It was a dual purpose, although many didn't realize its dual nature then. One part of the plan was that through the Jews the whole world should receive knowledge about God (in the Scriptures given them) and also deliverance from their rebellious natures. For through the Jewish bloodline God intended to come into the world Himself and, as a human being, to free men from the penalty and the power, and ultimately from the presence, of sin.

But most of Old Testament prophecy focused on God's plan for human life on this earth. Here the picture was broad and exciting to the Jewish believer. It showed that God intended to establish His personal authority over the earth. The Old Testament told the Jew that when God stepped into human history in human form, He would personally straighten out the confusion and misery we have caused. He would take over, enforcing righteousness. Things would be done God's way then, and peace and blessedness on earth would follow.

One of the things that always excited the Jews about this was the fact that their enemies, and all who lined up against their God, would be destroyed when the Messiah (for so the God-man is called) came. Then all who had trusted in Him, from every nation in the world, would be welcomed into His kingdom, and enjoy all the blessings God foretold of a time when rebellion simply would not be tolerated.

It was quite a hope. No matter how bad things seemed to be, the godly Jew knew that the world was not out of control. God was still in charge, and in His own time He would personally fashion of the warring kingdoms of this world one single, unified, peaceful kingdom of His own. The believing Jew knew that even if he did not see that kingdom in his day, it was surely coming. He knew too that if he and his neighbors lived in accordance with God's ways and in obedience to His laws, the same powerful God, who would some day step into history, would be watching and would see that they enjoyed the blessings of personal peace in their own lifetime.

So they had a big picture—the picture of a world under

control, the picture of human history with a purpose. No matter how successful sinful men and nations seemed, the misery they caused and the ultimate collapse of their hopes were simple demonstrations of the terribleness of sin, permitted so that men might discover how desperately they need God. No matter what men did, God's plan could not be shaken. His purpose was sure, and all of history moved on schedule toward the great culminating revelation of God Himself as the supreme and righteous Ruler of the earth.

The New Testament picture of God's plan

Jewish believers were shaken when Jesus, the Person they recognized as the Messiah of prophecy, was crucified. Even the resurrection, as exciting as this was, couldn't satisfy their wonder. What was happening to history? Why didn't Christ take His rightful place as King of the world, and put down all opposition? Was the plan revealed in the Old Testament changed?

The New Testament answer to this is: No, the Old Testament plan has not been changed. The Old Testament picture simply was not *complete*.

The Old Testament showed what the Messiah, Jesus, would do for the nation and the whole world. He still will do it. Everything that was written there will happen, just as described. But the New extends the Old Testament picture on past history into eternity. It shows us what will happen *after* the Old Testament portrait has been painted in time. One other thing—the New Testament focus shifts from God's plan for nations and peoples to His plan for individuals.

Part of this plan is to ultimately remove every last trace of our rebelliousness, bringing our personalities and motives into perfect harmony with His. This will happen at our resurrection when we believers will be restored to bodily life and fitted for eternity. So the New Testament big picture focuses our attention on heaven. It talks about our personal future and tells us of a never ending, always exciting eternal life with the Lord.

But part of God's planned solution to the sin problem is to begin the process of personality transformation right here on earth. Often the Bible talks about Christians as having a new life from God. A "share [in] God's essential nature," Peter calls it (2 Peter 1:4). And God intends that we actually live His kind of life right here in our sinful world. We're to be tugged at and pulled by all the temptations others feel; but, because we have God's life within us and because we see life from His point of view, we reject them all to live a truly *good* life. And, in living that kind of life, we show everyone around us how wonderful God is; we show them that even when the environment is against godly living, even when our rebellious inclinations are against godly choices, He is able to help us live above the sin around us and within.

A grasp of what God is doing, and how time is ultimately going to be swallowed up in eternity, is important to free us to live by "heavenly" rather than "earthly" values. Just as the godly Jew, the Christian has a conviction that God is in charge, that life does have a purpose and goal, and that we are invited to share in reaching those goals, certain all the time that what God has planned will happen—and happen to us!

And so life takes on new meaning.

So does the picture of the Old and New Testament of life fit together into one fully harmonious big picture. The Old Testament picture was correct as far as it went. The New Testament picture completes it by showing that *after* a time of personal rule on this earth, God will open up eternity to all who have believed in Him. Each believer resurrected and restored to full humanity, will share the destiny of eternal, conscious blessedness with God.

What of the earth itself? After the full drama of history is played out, the New Testament foretells the total destruction of this universe. The great reign of Christ as King is followed by one final rebellion, culminating in the dissolution of the very elements and atoms that compose this creation. Then, after a final judgment of all who have ever lived, God will re-create, making a new heaven and a new earth "in which nothing but good shall live" (2 Peter 3:13).

There are other ways that the Old and the New Testament fit together. One of the most important is that each focuses on Jesus Christ. In the Old, He is seen primarily as the coming King. In the New, He is seen primarily as the Savior, who freely forgives those who trust Him, and who works in our present lives to straighten out our warped personalities. In both Testaments He is central —the object and the Executor of God's plan.

And notice this: Each big picture, when understood and fully accepted in all its magnificent unlikeliness, *completely changes a person's understanding of life.* Seeing the big picture can have a fantastic impact on your values, on your evaluation of what really is important to you.

Getting your bearings

Sometimes sitting back and looking at the big picture gives us the idea that our present life is pretty insignificant—that our feelings and our problems, our doubts and our decisions, our times of happiness and triumph, really don't count for much. Maybe some Christians have taken it that way, and fallen into dreaming about "pie in the sky, by and by." But that's not what God intends.

In one place the Bible, after talking about our hope in heaven, hurries to say that this "doesn't, of course, mean that we only have a hope of future joys—we can be full of joy right here and now" (Rom. 5:3). So the here and now *is* important—both to us, and to God.

Why then the big picture? To help us get our bearings on life now.

This spring I spent some time fishing up in Wisconsin. There was one point off which the fishing was quite good—if you could find the right spot. But if I got out there in the lake, off that point, and just looked around at the water, I found no clue where that "right spot" was. What did I do? I looked off toward the shore, and lined myself up with landmarks I'd selected earlier. When I got those far-off landmarks in line, I knew I was in the right spot for good fishing.

Every single morning you and I set out on our "lake of life," and we need to find the right spot for ourselves— the spot where life takes on its fullest meaning and we experience the greatest joy. If we just look around our present situation for clues as to what to do, going by how we feel and what we want and what others think is best, we'll never find that spot. We need landmarks *outside* the situation—landmarks to line up our life by. This is just what God's big picture provides: landmarks—landmarks to help us get our bearings.

Remember Arlene, who found herself in a quickly developing, physically oriented relationship with her boyfriend? In that situation she was swayed by the pleasurable sensations she experienced. But when she looked outside the situation at her goals for her life, she got her bearings again. She decided that the goal of a Christian marriage was far more important than sexual stimulation now, and she began to act in a way that would help her move toward that goal.

That landmark made a lot of difference in her "here and now"!

A solid grasp on the landmarks God provides in His big picture can make the same kind of difference in *our* "here and now." It can change the way we evaluate our situations and the way we make our decisions. It can release us from the tyranny of all those false value systems we looked at earlier.

Have you been pinning your identity and your hopes on material possessions? Then realize that "the day of the Lord will come as suddenly and unexpectedly as a thief. In that day the heavens will disappear in a terrific tearing blast: the very elements will disintegrate in heat and the earth and all that is in it will be burned up to nothing" (2 Peter 3:10). So?

"In view of the fact that all these things are to be dissolved, what sort of people ought you to be? Surely men of good and holy character, who live expecting and earnestly longing for the coming of the day of God. True, this day will mean that the heavens will disappear in fire and the elements disintegrate in fearful heat, but our hopes are not set on these but on the new heavens and the new earth which he has promised us, and in which nothing but good shall live" (2 Peter 3:11-13).

Have you been dragged into a pattern of life by a desire to win the approval of others? Then here's something that can help you break free: "It is our aim" says Paul, "to please him, whether we are 'at home' [in our bodies] or 'away.' For every one of us will have to stand without pretense before Christ our judge, and we shall be rewarded for what we did when we lived in our bodies, whether it was good or bad" (2 Cor. 5:9-10). What if your friends think that the changes that living for God's approval make in your pattern of life are peculiar? "Don't worry: they are the ones who will have to explain their behavior before the one who is prepared to judge all men, whether living or dead" (1 Peter 4:5).

So the big picture can jolt us out of our provincial view of life, and help us put a lot of things in perspective.

This is just what we need to make our daily life vital, meaningful and full of joy: perspective.

We need landmarks—landmarks that help us keep our bearings in all the confusion of a struggling, seeking, unhappy humanity that truly does not know its way around life.

Steps to take

1. The impact of the big picture depends a lot on our grasp of it and our commitment to it. If you really bought all this, what changes do you think it might indicate in your pattern of life?

2. If you'd like to check out some Bible passages on this for yourself, why not take a look at these:
   Acts 1:1-8   Hebrews 11
   Romans 11   2 Peter 3
   2 Corinthians 5   Revelation 4–9
   2 Thessalonians 1

3. Look over the "Top-Ten" values list you just made up. How do these look to you in view of the big picture? Want to make any changes?

7

Fill "me" in

"My happiness affects my decisions very strongly," writes a college man. "I think that it is the most common end that I have in mind, consciously or unconsciously. Sometimes the other factors are used as a means to that end. For instance, I am inclined to seek God's will not for its own sake, but because I think I will be happier if I am living according to His will.

"As I get to know God better though, I find that I try to discover what He wants a little more often in order to please Him. It's a slow process, but even though my own happiness is still very important to me, *God's plan for me* is becoming more of an influence."

The big picture we looked at in the last chapter gives an overall perspective. But I need to know something about God's plan for *me*.

There's one thought in Romans 13 that I find really exciting: *"The present time is of the highest importance"* (v. 11). With all the sweeping grandeur of history, God has a purpose for you and for me, right now.

Lots of kids I talked with seemed impressed with the

idea of fitting into God's plan for them—someday. Like one guy who at fourteen was thinking hard about whether God wanted him to become an artist or a missionary pilot. "I have prayed about it," he says, "and talked to my dad, but as yet I haven't come to a conclusion." Man, has he missed the point! We fit into God's plan right now, and it's our *right now* that we're to concentrate on.

Here and now

The New Testament does more than outline God's overall plan. It fills in a lot of detail on how you and I fit in now. One passage in Titus sums up what is said in many places: "The grace of God, which can save every man, has now become known, and it teaches us to have no more to do with godlessness or the desires of this world but to live, here and now, responsible, honorable, and God-fearing lives" (Titus 2:11-12).

It's worth taking time to look at a few other passages that explain what God has in mind—particularly if you are like the Illinois high schooler who wrote, "I don't know if I *can* find any meaning in life. Life on the whole is not meaningful. I must find something extra." Get a firm grasp on God's viewpoint, and you'll find meaning where you least expect it!

Here are some passages that spell out that viewpoint for us.

"My brothers," writes Paul in one place, "we beg and pray you by the Lord Jesus, that you continue to learn more and more of the life that pleases God, the sort of life we told you about before. You will remember the instructions we gave you then in the name of the Lord Jesus. God's plan is to make you holy" (1 Thess. 4:1-3). Now, don't get the idea that "holiness" is a grim "I don't do *that"* kind of life. Paul outlines the Christian's holy life in some detail in his letter to the Romans: "Let us have no imitation Christian love. Let us have a genuine break with evil and a real devotion to good. Let us have a real warm affection for one another as between brothers, and a willingness to let the other man have the credit. Let us not allow slackness to spoil our work and let us keep the fires of the spirit burning, as we do our work for the Lord. Base your happiness on your hope in Christ. When trials come endure them patiently; steadfastly maintain the habit of prayer. Give freely to fellow Christians in want, never grudging a meal or a bed to those who need them. And as for those who try to make your life a misery, bless them. Don't curse them, bless. Share the happiness of those who are happy, the sorrow of those who are sad. Live in harmony with one another. Don't become snobbish but take a real interest in ordinary people. Don't become set in your own opinions. Don't pay back a bad turn by a bad turn, to *anyone*. See that your public behavior is above criticism. As far as your responsibility goes, live at peace with everyone. Never take vengeance into your own hands, my dear friends: stand back and let God punish if he will. For it is written: 'Vengeance belongeth unto me: I will recompense.' And these are God's words: 'If thine enemy hunger, feed him: If he thirst, give him to drink: For in so doing thou shalt heap coals of fire upon his head.' Don't allow yourself to be overpowered by evil. Take the offensive—overpower evil with good" (Rom. 12:9-21).

No wonder the Bible says that "the ultimate aim of the Christian ministry, after all, is to produce the love which springs from a pure heart, a good conscience and a genuine faith" (1 Tim. 1:5). Man, it takes a lot of love to live with others like this! But, as the Bible says, "This is your calling—to do good and one day to inherit all the goodness of God" (1 Peter 3:9*b*).

Now, this may seem like a mighty peculiar way to find meaning. Not in achieving, not in gaining, not in making a big name, not in doing—but in becoming a truly good person. But that is where the meaning is—in being "good" here and now—if you take God's view of life.

What does this do for that "happiness" motive that seems to move all of us these days? Several things. It shows us that happiness can never be found if we're looking for it as an end in itself. It isn't valid or valuable as a motive. But when you and I settle into God's pattern of goodness for our life, we'll find happiness as a by-product of the most peculiar circumstances.

Another look

I'm partial to basketball players. I enjoy the game so much that I usually get in an hour or two at our backyard ball-court every day. And I liked this basketball story from Ken, a nineteen-year-old Marylander.

"I decided to work hard at basketball, get good, and play for the team. I wanted this because it was enjoyable, and very important for social acceptance and popularity. I got good—and then tore ligaments in my knee just four days before my team tryouts! I tried out, but couldn't show my ability and was the last soph to be cut. Missing that year cost me a lot of experience. Though I made the team in my junior and senior years I was never really as effective as I'd expected.

"Less than a week *before* my knee injury, my pastor preached on priorities, values, and used the example of overemphasizing sports. He said that an athlete depended on 'the ligaments in one knee' for his 'security.' Then it happened!

"After that, basketball was mildly frustrating. It did make me more socially acceptable, but I began to value that differently. 'So-and-so is a Christian' means a lot more if he's on the high school team than if he's a 'Who's that?' The whole experience, painful as it was, was a key in switching my values from 'it's fun to be in' to 'it's effective for God.' "

So a painful experience began to look to Ken like a pretty good deal!

Ken's experience encourages us to take a second look at the "Let's do the happy thing" philosophy of life, and a second look at the Christian approach: "Let's do what's good and right." Even when the good and right may lead to painful experiences, the Christian who buys God's view of life prefers it. Someday, the Bible tells one group of Christians, you will be "able to pass through an [unhappy] experience and endure it with joy. You will even be able to thank God in the midst of pain and distress because you are privileged to share the lot of those who are living in the light" (Col. 1:11b-12). That second look at such experiences may even make us glad to have them!

Why? Because, just as torn ligaments helped Ken to develop a better set of values, every big and little tragedy can help us develop a better character and a better pattern of life. "When all kinds of trials and temptations crowd into your lives, my brothers, don't resent them as intruders, but welcome them as friends! Realize that they come to test your faith and to produce in you the quality of endurance. But let the process go on until that endurance is fully developed, and you will find that you have become men of mature character with the right sort of independence" (James 1:2-4).

This doesn't mean that we go around looking for trou-

ble. But we don't try to dodge difficulties by taking the easy way out. We look for the right thing to do, the good thing to do, and willingly accept whatever results this way of life may bring.

Now, all this may very well seem "way out" to you. Particularly if you're having a hard time right now. When everything seems to be going wrong, you're being treated unfairly by your parents or your friends or your teachers, or by life in general, the idea that "It's good for me" is pretty hard to take. You might even feel like slugging anyone who says it! God realizes this. "Obviously," He says, "no 'chastening' seems pleasant at the time: it is in fact most unpleasant. Yet when it is all over we can see that it has quietly produced the fruit of real goodness in the characters of those who have accepted it in the right spirit" (Heb. 12:11). And that's worth a lot. To God, anyway.

And so we're right back where we started. Looking for the meaning of life? As a Christian, "real goodness" of character and life is God's purpose for you "here and now."

Real goodness is where it's at.

And real goodness is where we'll be at when we learn to fit into life in God's way.

Real goodness

What about "real goodness"?

First, we'd better go back to those dos and don'ts lists—to say right out that they have very little to do with real goodness—very little. Christians have always disagreed about various social practices. In Bible days some said you shouldn't eat meat purchased at temple meat markets. Other said "A steak is a steak!" Some felt certain days were more important than others, while another group considered all days alike. How does the Bible handle such quibbling? By making room for differing convictions. "Let every one be definite in his own convictions. If a man specially observes one particular day, he does so 'to the Lord.' The man who eats eats 'to the Lord,' for he thanks God for the food. The man who fasts also does it 'to the Lord,' for he thanks God for the benefits of fasting. The truth is that we neither live nor die as self-contained units. At every turn life links us to the Lord, and when we die we come face to face with him. In life or death we are in the hands of the Lord. Christ lived and died that he might be the Lord in both life and death" (Rom. 14:5b-9).

What does this mean? That each of us is to look to Jesus

Christ as Lord of our life, and to do what we feel Christ wants. We are each to live as personally responsible to God.

Actually, the Bible doesn't make a lot over this question, because real goodness can never be summed up in lists of things that we do or don't do. The Bible seems to mention them only because such lists can get in the way of goodness! How? Romans goes on to show that sometimes we let our personal convictions so affect our attitudes toward others that we fail to apply the really important values in living with them. Do the things on their lists, or things on yours, lead you to criticize them, to make them look small? Does your insistence that you are free from such lists lead you to feel free of your obligation to love your critics, to care for them so much that you even give up your "rights" for the sake of harmony? No, real goodness ought to be so important to us that our little differences are swallowed up in mutual love.

When we think about practicing mutual love, we're getting back to where the Bible says life is at for us, here and now. We're getting back to real goodness. Look over this list of what is important to God, (it's from that long passage in Romans 12 quoted earlier) and see how love works out in practice:

a genuine break with evil
a real devotion to good
a real warm affection for one another as between brothers
willingness to let the other man have the credit
no laziness to spoil our work
enduring trials patiently
giving freely to Christians in want
never grudging a meal or a bed to those who need them

blessing, not cursing, those who try to make our life a
    misery
sharing the sorrow and happiness of others
living in harmony with one another
not being snobbish, but taking a real interest in ordi-
    nary people
not paying back a bad turn, to anyone
even going as far as to feed and care for your enemy
    when he's in trouble

Beside *this* list, all those little dos and don'ts that
Christians sometimes make such a fetish of seem down-
right petty. To God the "great commandment" is first to
love Him and then to love our neighbor. The Bible talks
about a "perpetual debt of love which we owe one
another," and shows that when we act in love, all lists are
superseded. "Love hurts nobody: therefore love is the
answer to the Law's commands" (Rom. 13:8, 10). And
love in action is exactly what we see described in portraits
of real goodness.

The exciting thing is, a person doesn't have to wait for
adulthood to live this kind of life. It's open to everyone,
right now. "There's this girl in the dorm," says a fifteen-
year-old from California, "who'd let anyone (I mean the
kids) rule over her. She was too humble and had a terrible
inferiority complex. Because of her actions, we all bossed
her around and let her do our jobs for us, partly because
she seemed to want to do our jobs. I finally realized that
this kid needed help and we were doing the opposite for
her. So I had to make myself stop, and to begin treating
her like I treated everyone else, because it was right."
Know something? When she did that little thing, she
began fitting into God's purpose. She was living a meaningful life, here and now.

One young Illinois girl sent me a little diagram (Fig. 2) with this comment: "Maybe you could mention, or give answer to, why so many kids pick on the more unnoticed or less popular or 'way out' kids, in an attempt to higher themselves. In reality, although they have succeeded in lowering someone else, they haven't themselves moved up a bit." She's right. Trying to build yourself up at someone's expense never works out. Jesus put it this way:

> "You know that the so-called rulers in the heathen world lord it over them, and their great men have absolute power. But it must not be so among you. No, whoever among you wants to be great must become the servant of you all, and if he wants to be first among you he must be the slave of all men! (Mark 10:42-44).

The way a Christian raises himself is to lower himself and to serve others!

Figure 2

One may feel lower, but the person who puts others down hasn't moved up a bit!

Now, all this may seem a bit upside down. Breaking with everything evil, willingness to let the other guy get the credit, rejecting snobbishness for a real interest in ordinary people, and never paying back a bad turn just isn't the way the world runs. Most people expect to dabble in evil just a little bit to get ahead. After all, what's a fellow going to do if the coach tells an off-color joke? Look away? And who's going to make points if he lets someone else get the credit? If we never pay back a bad turn, won't other people run all over us? And surely if you're going to be somebody you have to cultivate the kids who are in, and ignore the ordinary Joes just like they do. Don't you?

Not if you buy God's values and decide to lay out your life in the pattern He shows us.

What seems important to Him may not look important to other people. But if we're looking for meaning in life, it's just that aspect that has to become important to us.

Off the fence

Way back at the beginning of this book I suggested that too many of us drift through life, controlled by values that we're not even aware of. And I said that rather than let ourselves be controlled, we'd better step up and take control of our own lives.

Now we're getting toward the place where we have enough information to jump down off that fence and take a stab at control. Remember how we got here? In chapters 2–4 we looked at some of the hidden values that often slip up on us and dictate our decisions. Maybe you saw some of them struggling to control you. Or maybe not. In chapter 5 we thought about the nature of values and saw how they reflect our view of the meaning of life. We saw how "What's important to me?" shapes the pattern of our lives by focusing attention on some factors in a situation and blocking out others, and by predisposing us to accept some reasons for actions while rejecting others. So we need to test values to measure what seems important against what *is* important.

It's clear by now that I'm personally convinced that in the Bible God reveals the meaning of life. Its big picture tells us His overall plan and gives us landmarks to keep in sight, always. Besides this, every book and chapter, particularly of the New Testament, help to fit "me" in this picture. They give God's viewpoint on what is important in human life: they tell me why I'm here, and how my life can be meaningful to me as I live it and, in the long run, through eternity.[1]

An issue that faces us now that we understand how values affect our lives and how to check out our values against God's is How do we get off the fence and take control of life? How do we begin to live "with a due sense of responsibility, not as men who do not know the meaning and purpose of life, but as *those who do*"?

There aren't any easy answers to this. We'll look at some of the problems young people have found and some of the questions they ask in the last three chapters. But just knowing what we do right now, several clear courses of action are open.

Get God's values in focus. This takes digging into the Bible—the right way. By this I mean, don't go looking for a lot of hard and fast rules. There are some absolutes in Scripture, of course. Some things are *never* right. But these are few. There is far more about the kind of persons God wants us to be: the character traits that are important to Him, and the patterns of life that constitute true goodness.

There are other ways to read the Bible, and other things

to look for, of course.[2] But, to make sure that what's important to you is really what is important, there's no substitute for searching God's Word.

Apply these values daily. Remember that "true goodness" relates primarily to interpersonal relationships—to living out love with others. Right now you probably aren't a missionary, and can't do any of the "big" things for God that some people dream of. But you sure have contact with people! At home, at school, at church, on your athletic team, in your neighborhood, all over the place. The fact is that this makes the Christian life a "here and now" thing for you. Every person you know provides an opportunity to live love.

This isn't easy for any of us. Life seldom makes a complete turnabout so that suddenly we see and feel about and do everything God's way. God knows that, and you should too. In one place the Bible talks about the Christian life as "sharing the miracle of rising again to new life" (Col. 2:12). It doesn't say that we "have risen." It says "rising." Life on earth is a process for us—a process of sharing more and more of Christ's life, and becoming more and more like Him.

So it doesn't pay to get discouraged if we seem to fumble our attempts. But it does pay to *start.*
After all, it is your life.
You've got the opportunity to take control, today.

Steps to take

1. Here are some Scripture portions you might want to think through; they say a lot about values and the "truly good" life:

Mark 2:1–3:7	2 Corinthians 8-9
John 13:1-18	Philippians 2
Romans 13	Ephesians 4:17–6:19

2. Here's a way to check out your pattern of personal relationships. Each morning for a week read 1 Corinthians 13 and relate it to a different person or group you are close to. Whenever you see a way to put the love it describes into practice, do it.

3. Yep, you guessed it. Go over the "Top-Ten" again. (It's the last time, honest.) In view of what you've read and what you've discovered in the Scriptures, want to make any changes?

8

The right thing

A New Jersey college girl warns, "All formulas, rules and regulations should be left unsaid. All decisions depend to some extent on the individual and the situation and his relationship to God. There are no pat answers."

The more you run across this kind of thinking, the more you begin to wonder if it's ever possible to know the right thing.

Say you're sitting down, about to take a test, and in come two kids. One is a good friend of yours who has been sick and just got back to school. The other is a loud-mouth you don't like at all, and you know he spends all his time running around with low-rep girls. The first sits down tiredly on your right; the second swaggers over to the seat on your left. Then, this guy on your left tugs your sleeve and says, "Hey man, how 'bout lettin' me copy off your paper today? I was [smirk] out late last night." What's likely to be your first thought about that? No! Cheating isn't right.

But a minute later your buddy on the right tugs your

sleeve and says, ''Can you help me out just this once? I felt too sick last night to study, and I'm so far behind. I just have to pass this test.'' Now what's your first thought? About friendship? Or maybe how deserving he is?

In the first case there doesn't seem to be a value conflict. The first character who asks you to cheat doesn't deserve

help. He's in a bind because of his own actions and his own wrong choices. Some nerve to try to get you to do something against the rules to help him out of the hole he dug by himself!

But in the second case, most of us would feel some inner conflict. There's the feeling that somehow cheating isn't right, and the feeling that helping out a friend is a good thing to do, particularly when that friend is deserving and has a special need. In this case, wouldn't "the loving thing to do" be to help him out?

Easy does it

I hope you didn't get the idea from the last two chapters that once a person straightens out his values, life suddenly becomes simple, that decision-making is a breeze. One collegian said, "I don't think you'll advise kids just to 'seek God's will, not what the crowd wants' and expect all the answers to appear—it's too easy, too pat, and certainly doesn't aid decision-making. And I think we do need help. It seems to me that a lot of kids from Christian backgrounds are so used to having parents and church dictate that even when we reach college we are incapable of making decisions."

Actually, high schoolers today make far more unsupervised decisions than at any other time in our history. More than one writer talks about the "increasing social liberation of adolescents," with "the increasing inability of parents to enforce norms—about hours at night, conditions of dating, etc.—constraining their teenagers' behavior."[1] As a consequence, young people today, says a sociologist James S. Coleman, show a greater tendency to "disregard adult dictates, to consider themselves no longer subject to the demands of parents and teachers, and to pay less and less attention to the prescribed scholastic 'exercises.' "[2] Plainly put, this means that you feel, and take, much more responsibility for decisions than teens did in my day, and have much more free time when adults aren't "watching" than I ever did.

One popular ethical system says that "end" values (like love) are the *only* values that ought to be used in making a decision. That is, in any given situation you calculate the probable results of your actions and choose to do what will be best for the persons involved. Does this work? Let's see by trying it in the cheating case above.

In the first place, the new moralist, like the collegian quoted at the beginning of the chapter, would say "all formulas, rules and regulations should be left unsaid." So we will not say anything about cheating being right or wrong. To this way of thinking, its rightness and wrongness depend completely on whether cheating helps or hinders us from doing the "loving" thing—what's best for our friend. So, from this point of view, our *only* consideration is, Will cheating to help our friend, actually help him, or harm him?

How can we tell? By projecting the possible *results* of the different options we have. Say that we decide *not* to help him. What are the results?

a. He might pass the test anyway.
b. He might fail the test.

Now, is this helpful or harmful to him? We really can't tell until we know the results of *this*. Here we can dismiss the first result (*a*) from our calculations because, supposedly, if he passes the test, he wouldn't have needed our help. The long-term results would seem to be the same no matter what we do. But if he fails the test, a variety of things might result:

1. He might have to repeat the subject in summer school to graduate.
2. He might become so discouraged he drops out of high school.
3. He might have to repeat the whole grade and graduate a year late.
4. He might be rejected by the college he wants to go to because of low marks.
5. He might go to see the teacher, explain, and be given a makeup test.

Now, none of these is, in itself, either good or bad. Why? Because we can't tell beforehand the result of *these* outcomes. If we turn our imaginations loose we can project all sorts of things that *might* happen as a result of each of these five possible outcomes of failing the test. Let's try it—imagining, but foreseeing nothing that isn't *possible*.

1. Jack (let's call him Jack) flunks and has to repeat the subject in summer school. He turns down a great summer job that would have paid off most of his first year of college. Discouraged, he's influenced by some of the guys in summer school to try pot. Soon he goes on to harder stuff, till he's mainlining heroin. He dies in an institution at the age of twenty-two—all because *you* wouldn't cheat to help him pass an insignificant little test!

Don't like that? Well, try this: Jack goes to summer school and turns down that fantastic job. Later he learns that everyone who took it was killed when a charter bus the group was traveling in went off the road in the Rockies. And at school he meets Karil in a class they take together. Three years later they're married, and Karil works to put him through medical school. When their first child is born five years after this, they name him after you!

2. Jack drops out and doesn't finish high school. He tries to find a job, but no one wants him, so he sponges off his folks for several years. With nothing to do, he sits around the house and drinks beer. He gets fat and sloppy. Finally his dad, who's disgusted with him, kicks him out. In a fit of drunken rage, Jack burns down the house and kills his parents. Now aren't you sorry!

No? How about this: Unable to get a job, Jack decides to go it on his own. Always a science-fiction bug, he thinks he'll try to write some. After a few rejection slips Jack sells his first short story to *Astounding Science Fiction* magazine. With added confidence he digs in enthusiastically, and in ten years becomes the best known and wealthiest science-fiction writer around. Not only that, but in researching for his fantasies he comes up with ideas for future scientific discoveries (as have Jules Verne and others!). Convinced that some of his projections are workable, he invests his writing profits in a small laboratory, and hires two brilliant young Ph.D.'s to develop his ideas. Out of this lab come the first ion space drive, and even an antigravity machine. These make possible visiting and exploring the whole solar system.

Man, just think how awful it would have been if you'd helped him on that test!

3. Jack has to repeat the whole grade. He's unhappy about it at first, but later he learns that repeating it means he graduates just when the government gives all high school grads a free college education. If he'd graduated with *you* he'd have had to pay for his education.

4. Jack is turned down by the college he has set his heart on, and decides to go to a small junior college nearby. There he's influenced by a small group of student rebels, and leads a march on the college president's

house. Lighting a bomb he intends to throw at the police, he miscalculates. It goes off and blinds him.

Too gory? Jack is turned down by the college he has set his heart on, and decides to go to a small junior college nearby. There he's influenced by a professor he meets and becomes interested in camping and forestry. Jack changes his vocational plans, and goes on to live an exciting and happy life supervising one of our new national park areas near Lake Superior.

Or this: Jack decides to spend a year at a Bible college while waiting to enter next year's class at the college of his choice. The Lord uses friends and courses there to lead him into missions. He goes on to translate the Scriptures into the languages of no less than three large tribal groups, earns his Ph.D. in linguistics, and sees 97,999 of the pagan tribespeople become Christians.

I could go on. So could you. *Because almost anything, good or bad, that we can imagine might possibly result from failing that test!*

At any point, life opens up in a myriad of directions, and any one of dozens of turning points can alter our future. With life as complex as it is, the idea that we can actually calculate the results of any given action is simply foolish!

Oh, we can make educated guesses and often hit the *near* results. That is, in the test situation with Jack, you can predict that he will pass it or fail it, depending on what you do. But what will passing or failing *ultimately* mean? We can't even begin to guess.

At best, we can only see the edge of tomorrow.

The suggestion that we make decisions with reference only to love is an empty one. We need more than a motive of love and a desire to help in order to make *good* decisions.

Full speed ahead

Probably most decisions we make aren't exactly life-shattering. It's like one nineteen-year-old describes high school life:

"I don't think my decisions were made on a day-to-day basis but rather in terms of an enduring commitment, or in terms of responsibilities I felt. These dictated my daily activities.

"To start with, I was a student, planning to go to college, so I didn't decide whether to study or not to study, I just knew I had to. Study came before leisure. No decision.

"Then there was my responsibility to the Lord. As a Christian I felt responsible to go to church Sunday morning and evening, and Wednesday, and there was never any decision to be made then. When there were extra things, I went to them too. Studies and church held first place in my activities. There was never any conflict of whether to study or go to church. I could always handle both without choosing. These two things were my primary responsibilities.

"Beyond that, I made decisions or commitments, and these usually determined long-range, day-to-day decisions. For example, I joined the band. When there was band practice or a parade or football game, I knew I had to be there. No decision on my part. The same with the yearbook—when a deadline was coming up, the work had to be done and I didn't decide whether I'd do it or not. Deciding to join the organization made day-to-day decision unnecessary.

"What made me decide to join organizations? Mostly my enjoyment of the activity. I was lousy in band and on the field hockey team, but I joined because I had fun. I

enjoyed the activity and enjoyed being with the group."
And so life went on.

Really, each day of a person's life isn't filled with all
sorts of tough, value-conflict decisions. Probably ninety-
nine percent of our choices aren't determined by a special
"today" decision but by our habits of living. This is important to note. Why? Because it emphasizes something
we looked at earlier: *the pattern of our lives*. It's the *pattern*
that reflects values, and it's the pattern we need to check.
How do you respond to your younger brother and sister?
In the habit of nagging and criticizing them all the time?
Then you don't *decide* each time you jump on their back;
it's become your way of living with them. And this
doesn't square with God's intention for your life and
character! So you need to deal with the pattern of life,
check over what is really important to you and God in
your relationships, and consciously change your re-
sponses until this new way becomes your pattern of life.

Also, much of our life pattern is ethically and morally
neutral. By that I mean it isn't related to values. It simply
relates to our interests, and likes and dislikes. You like to
wear red socks all the time? Great. Don't get concerned
about whether this is God's will or not. Your choice of
socks doesn't say anything about your values. All it says
is that you like red.

Does one of your friends like to read science stuff, while
you prefer historical novels? OK. Feel free. Develop your
own interests without a nervous flip over what this means
concerning your values. It doesn't mean anything. You
have one set of interests, and he has another. After all,
God can (and probably will) use each set of interests to
develop each of you as a unique personality.

What if you get up at 5 A.M. to study while someone else
studies all night? Don't sweat it; there's room for indi-

vidual differences. This kind of thing just doesn't relate to values.

So live most of life full speed ahead. But slow down if you catch a pattern that is out of harmony with what's important to God. And slow down and think seriously when you begin to wonder about a particular decision, when you hit that percentage of life when you aren't sure what's the right thing to do.

Several times I've used the words *value conflict* to describe a situation like this—when inside you feel uncertain about the right thing to do. There are some other situations that might masquerade as value conflict, but aren't.

Not every time you hesitate over a decision will "value conflict" be the reason. Sometimes the conflict will be between what we *want* to do and what we're sure is the right thing to do.

"My first date," relates an Illinois girl, "occurred in the middle of my senior year. I had been a Christian about a year when this (1) non-Christian guy asked me out on (2) a Sunday evening to (3) a dance! My answer was no because my church frowned on especially (1) and (3). Since that was my only argument, he broke through after about six or seven no's. He was quite persistent. Before the night was over I had not only learned how to dance but a little about the art of 'making love' as well. I was too curious to know what it was all about to stop, even though I knew through instinct and the Bible that it wasn't right."

This wasn't a value conflict. This was a conflict between her values and her curiosity. And she went a lot further than she's happy about, because she shoved her values aside and let her curiosity take over.

But there are definite value conflicts at other times—

times when we have to choose between two things, both of which seem "right." Like that cheating episode. It's right to be honest and not cheat. And yet, it's also right to help a friend. How do you decide in a case like this? What "in situation" guidelines can we look for?

Ends and means

When Jack asked for help, the value conflict that arose was between an *end value* and a *means value*. That is, helping a friend in need is a good thing, and it's a desirable end to wish him well. We ought to work for his good. But just a moment's thought indicates that the value "don't cheat" has nothing to do with ends. That's a value that says something about how to achieve an end.

Most rules are like this. They concern means, and are not ends in themselves. For instance, *why* "don't cheat"? Because we're concerned with a particular end—being fair to everyone—and cheating isn't. It isn't fair to the kids who do study. It isn't fair to the cheater, because taking this kind of shortcut is likely to get him out of the habit of honest preparation. It isn't fair to the college or future employer, because they look at a person's record and act as if it reflects his achievement. It really isn't fair to anyone. So the rule "don't cheat" is a *means* to "provide fair treatment for everyone involved" (*the end*).

What happens when an *end* value comes into conflict with a *means* value? Either a person thinks the normal means will not lead to the desired end, or he thinks a *higher* end involved takes priority. In our cheating illustration, the end of helping our friend might seem more important *in this situation* than the general end of being fair to everyone. And when this happens, a person feels a value bind.

Lots of people today say that *end* values are the only

significant ones, and in cases like these the thing to do is throw out the *means* values and forget them. They feel that the only thing that's important is to do what's good for the other guy. To the person who says, "Toss over all the rules and act only on *end* values," we have to reply, "Sounds nice, but it won't work." As we've seen, we can never *know* ahead of time the actual results of an action. So we can't just "do what works out for the best." We need some way of knowing *what* will work out for the best.

If a person says, "Yeah, but here in the situation I can make a better guess as to results than some rule maker who isn't here," we have to reply, "That depends."

And it does—on who makes those rules, and on what our world is really like.

In charge

Have you ever wondered why a God who values *love* supremely, and cares intensely about the good of His children, should make rules? You should. Because the Bible does contain rules, and suggests that we keep them! "In practice," the Bible says, "the more a man learns to obey God's laws, the more truly and fully does he express his love for him. Obedience is the test of whether we really live 'in God' or not" (1 John 2:5). What are some of these rules? Well, here's a tough one:

Subject yourself to authority.

That one hurts, doesn't it. "Obey the authorities," the Bible says of civil government, "not simply because it is the safest, but because it is the right thing to do" (Rom. 13:5). This principle is applied throughout Scripture to all sorts of relationships. To parents, if you're a teen. To "every man-made authority," to say nothing of employees accepting the authority of their bosses.

What about unjust authorities? Well, in the New Testament, slaves are told to "submit to your masters with proper respect—not only to the good and kind, but also to the difficult" (1 Peter 2:18). If the person in authority acts wrongly, it's really not an excuse for your breaking loose.

Many people wonder about this kind of rule, and they honestly feel that they should break rules when they seem to stand in the way of achieving important ends. I'd probably wonder too if I weren't a Christian and didn't have a peculiar perspective on all such statements of *means*.

And that perspective?

Remember a phrase from a passage I quoted earlier? Something about life linking us at every turn to the Lord? And that "in life or death we are in the hands of the Lord"? Well, that word *Lord* makes all the difference. It means more than giving our lives to Christ to control. It asserts that Jesus Christ is *in control* of everything. He is "head of *everything* for the church." He's in charge. Christ's lordship means that *He can make sure the means He has established will really work*. The means He has established will *always* work out to achieve His ends for His children. You see, the biblical God isn't an absentee landlord; He's not just an interested bystander. He's really in charge. And He is the One who supervises the results of all our choices.

A while ago I pointed out that you and I can never tell beforehand what will really help. We can't be sure that the end we have in mind will actually come to pass, so we need guidelines to tell us what will really help others and not harm them. You know, if I point a gun at someone and pull the trigger, not knowing it is loaded and not wanting to harm him, it can kill him anyway. Good motives don't always make that much difference in our actions either! What we do from a desire to help may actually harm if we do the wrong thing.

See what this says about our choice of means? It says that in making choices we not only have to consider the end we have in view, but we also have to consider the means that we expect to achieve the end. Here the Christian has a dual advantage over the non-Christian. He realizes that those rules, which some people so greatly despise (and here I mean rules given in Scripture), provide us with the very means we need to *do good* to others. And the Christian knows why they *work* that way!

This is what was behind that little problem I raised in chapter 5—and didn't try to solve. Remember? About lying for a friend. Would you do it? I wouldn't. Not if I really cared about him and wanted to do him good. The Bible says, "Don't tell one another lies any more" (Col. 3:9), and that cuts off the lie forever as a means I can use to "help" anyone!

Does this seem foolish? Maybe you've told a lie and found it helped you out of a tight spot. Doesn't prove a thing. Maybe God wanted you *in* that tight spot. It might have improved your character! Maybe God wanted you to learn that He could get you out of that spot without lies. When you took the wrong way out, you cut yourself off forever from discovering just what God hoped to accomplish in your life.

No, the Christian can feel free to keep the rules about means because he knows that God made them, and that God Himself is in charge, making sure His purposes are realized in our right decisions.

This is really what value conflict often boils down to. We want to do a good thing—a helpful, loving thing— and we see a rule that seems to stand in the way. Don't lie. Don't rebel against authority. Don't cheat. And because the end we have in mind seems so much more important and valuable than the rule, we break it. We lie. We rebel. We cheat. And we call it "good."

That's not what the Bible calls it. And besides that, the Bible might well name it "foolish." For certainly the God good enough to give us a desire to love and help others is also wise enough to show us *how* we can actually be helpful!

The rules God gives us don't hinder us from doing good. They don't replace the *end* values the Bible shows us are so important. But they do show us the only way we can really do good. And breaking these rules, even for the sake of good motives, is *never* the right thing to do.

So value conflict really focuses our attention on something we didn't suspect was the issue: *Can we trust God?* Is God a Person who is truly interested and involved in our lives? Does He, as the Bible claims, really supervise the results of our choices and our actions? Can He, as Lord of this world, make sure that His good follows when we do the right thing?

No matter how you cut it, that's how this whole issue of value conflicts has to be resolved.—by asserting that God is Lord.

And that *His* rules are means that lead to good, helpful and loving ends.

Steps to take

1. Check your understanding of this chapter by jotting down your meaning for the following words and phrases. Then check through the chapter again to see how close your definitions are to the author's.

Value conflict	End values	Lord
Rules	Means	

2. In the last chapter you looked through some Scripture passages to find and list some "end" values. Can you find three more "means" values besides the ones the author mentions in the text?

3. How about your relationship with your parents? Or with other authorities? Or how you handle tough spots? How would your pattern of life be affected by a conviction that God will take care of the results when you do the right thing?

9

God's will

"I think it is important to emphasize that decisions should be well thought out," says a fellow from Iowa. "But when you have investigated the possibilities and you still must make a decision between two seemingly good alternatives (from what you can tell), then you must take a plunge by making your own decision."

And this is something else again. Here we can't tell what to do by looking at the big picture. We can't even decide by looking for rules. Here we have to look for something Christians usually call "God's will."

How many decisions do you hesitate over that seem to have nothing to do with values? Probably most involve choices where one isn't "good" and the other isn't "bad." Probably most of your decisions don't even involve keeping or breaking rules—God's or man's.

The fellows and girls who helped me with his book were really concerned about decisions just like this.

"Once when my family and I were on vacation out of town," says a fifteen-year-old Californian, "I had a decision of staying in this place with some friends, and doing some work at this friend's business, or going on with my family. I knew I wanted to go home and be with my family, but I also wanted to stay for two reasons. One, I wanted to work, and two, there was a girl there—need I say more? Well, I decided to stay and fly home in a few weeks."

"I was accepted at two colleges and was faced with a decision of which one I should go to. I prayed about it and discussed it with my parents. Both colleges had advantages and disadvantages but, as time passed, one seemed to me to stand out over the other."

"I took typing because I felt it would help me in the rest of school," says a fifteen-year-old. "I am taking PE as well as being a PE aid next year because I enjoy this kind of thing and may be a PE teacher as my life work."

And, asks a girl from Idaho, "What about a guy and girl that feel they were meant to be married, but one was going to be a missionary? Should they separate because of their different duties to the Lord?"

None of these situations can be solved by applying rules. No rules exist that apply! To make this kind of decision, we leave all rules behind. This is important to get straight. Life *isn't* by rule. For most of life, and for most decisions, rules simply will not apply.

Now, this doesn't contradict anything we saw last chapter. There I suggested that certain *rules about means* should never be broken, and that no circumstances ever make lying or rebelliousness "the right thing to do." As Christians we can feel free to make "our sole defense, our only weapon . . . a life of integrity" (2 Cor. 6:8) because God is in charge, and makes sure that these rules really work. But please do not take this thinking about rules out of the context of right and wrong *means*. Don't think that there are all sorts of rules that govern our lives, and that if we just find the right rule we can make any possible decision "by the book." It's not true. Most of our decisions concern issues for which there is no rule.

Like, which college to go to. Which high school courses to take. Which person to marry. What vocation to choose. Whether to go here for a vacation, or there. To take a summer job, or a trip with the family. For making decisions like these, rules won't help. You need personal, not general, guidance.

Here is where Christians begin to talk about "God's will for my life," and where many feel that they need God's help and guidance. "I'd like help to learn God's will for my life," says a fifteen-year-old from California.

And a Texas girl says, "I think God's will for a Christian's life should be stressed because of its importance. Before my parents became missionaries, they pastored, and I remember many times when they were in the Lord's will, and how God blessed them tremendously for obeying. Such a wonderful peace comes from knowing you are in God's will."

Most of us have the idea from Scripture that God has a plan for our life, and a wonderful future mapped out for us. "I will instruct you and teach you in the way you should go: I will counsel you and watch over you," the Bible says (Ps. 32:8 NIV), and goes on to tell us not to act like a wild horse that has to be pulled into the right path with a painful bit and bridle. We are to let God give us His individual guidance. The New Testament even suggests that God has placed His hand on us Christians and remade us as "his workmanship, created in Christ Jesus to do those good deeds which God planned for us to do" (Eph. 2:10). No wonder we have the idea that God intends to guide us through life. Also, we have a promise that if, in the process of life "any of you does not know how to meet any particular problem he has only to ask God—who gives generously to all men without making them feel foolish or guilty—and he may be quite sure that the necessary wisdom will be given him" (James 1:5).

So life does link us "at every turn" with the Lord, and the Lord stands ready at each turning point to show us which is His best way for us.

"But"

"I know in my case," says a high school girl, "I have wanted to make good decisions, but I don't know how." That's a mighty big "but"! Personal guidance? How does it work?

A twenty-one-year-old California girl illustrates the confusion most of us have felt: "Include a discussion of the will of God," she asks. "Am I trying to discover a predetermined blueprint for my life? The one place God wants me to be at a particular time? The husband God has chosen for me? Any number of situations where God can teach me things and where He can use me? Can I say that it's God's will that I go to one school and not another? Is there one man God has chosen for me? Or are there several with whom I am compatible? If I happen to go one place, I'll meet one; but if I go somewhere else, I'll meet another."

Yes, life is complex. And decisions like these have life-shaping impact. No wonder so many ask if there really is a "one-way" sign attached to life—a blueprint that maps out our whole future; one He expects us to follow.

I think the Scriptures we looked at a moment ago show us a plan does exist. But that doesn't mean we can know it "all at once."

What do I mean? That "knowing God's will" doesn't mean a revelation of His total plan for our life. It means knowing what He wants us to do *now*. This is why I said earlier that the fourteen-year-old who was trying to decide if God wants him to be an artist or missionary pilot has missed the point. You don't find out something like this that far ahead of time. God's will—as we can know it—and His guidance—as we can experience it—relate to right now, not to tomorrow. I can have God's help in making decisions that face me today, but I really can't know what tomorrow will hold until it comes.

"I do honestly want God's will, and I pray about it," says a high school sophomore, "but it doesn't seem to do much good. It seems like my prayers just go up to the ceiling." Maybe he's made just the mistake we're talking about by praying, "Lord, tell me your *long-range* plans for me." And God simply doesn't do this.

In practice, confidence that we know what God intends for us tomorrow can get us into an unhappy bind. Like the girl who always figured God's plan for her was to marry the guy she'd dated steadily for three years: "In the third year we dated, I began to evaluate our relationship and I discovered that I really didn't love him. It was oh so hard to break up, because we had been going together for so long and people assumed we were really in love. But I knew that I could not marry except for love. In my mind I valued a marriage filled with God-given love, and I wanted only what God wanted for me. So I broke up the relationship. I was lonely for two years. But now God has honored the value I respected, and soon I will be married to the one I truly love and the one who loves me."

The feeling that she knew God's "long-range" plan made her feel bound to a guy who wasn't God's man for her at all! That's the main drawback to the "long-range" idea. Just see what's happened to this Idaho girl: "I knew the Lord wanted me to be a missionary, but I wasn't willing to face up to it. I kept saying I'd go to Bible school and from there the Lord would show me, but now there is no turning back. I've clearly seen that He wants me on the mission field and I've made an open profession of it. If I did turn back it would shame my Lord terribly and I couldn't do that and be able to live."

Now, I'm not critical of her for facing up to her conviction that God wants her on the mission field, or for openly saying "I'll go." Being willing and telling others we're willing are important for all of us. But how about this "now there's no turning back" idea? Can't she ever again listen to what God might say? Not even if later God shows her something else?

It does happen, you know. I came to know the Lord while in the navy, and the conviction grew that God wanted me in the ministry. I finished college after my discharge and went off to seminary. There I prepared to be a pastor. In fact, on our graduation night I spoke representing the future pastors in my class! Two weeks later I was working as a writer with a Sunday school publishing house. Three years after that I began to teach at Wheaton College. I've never been a pastor. And I *know* that God has sovereignly guided me into each of these ministries.

What if, because I once felt called to a pastoral ministry and acted on that call by going to seminary, I had refused to listen when God showed me what He really intended? What if I blocked off all His *present* communication and present guidance, insisting that God is not free to show me something I haven't known before? Pretty foolish, isn't it?

And tragic. Because it's guidance *today* we always need and must seek.

This is what a Connecticut girl finally decided. "I have wanted God's will, at least deep down, since not long after I was saved. But I was mixed up, and operated more out of habit than anything else; even coming to college was something I did because I'd always planned to, without much thought. This summer I realized it was about time to bring God into the picture and earnestly seek His will in regard to my major, among other things. I prayed quite a bit about it and then logically thought through the pros and cons and plans for courses for several majors. By the end of the summer I was certain, and peaceful about it, that biology would be the most practical major, at least for now. It meant I had to change my major and drop one course and take another. I prayed all would go well if it were God's will. Everything did."

See what she's saying? *Now* when we face a decision we need to bring God into the question and ask Him about it. When we're peaceful and confident about the choice, we make it "at least for now." And so we leave life open to God, and we stay willing to listen when He has future changes to suggest.

That's the kind of guidance God is willing to give.

And when we're ready to take it this way, we've come a long way toward living by faith.

Magic? Hardly

Experiencing God's day-by-day guidance isn't magic and isn't "supernatural"—in the sense of getting telegrams from heaven. Everything we've discussed so far helps us to build a picture of the way God guides us—the way we can experience His direction. Let's review what's involved.

Motives and values. This is the big, basic thing. Is what's important to you really important to God? "In high school I ran for several offices to *be* somebody. I wanted to be president of the band or on student council, not for any reason like service, but just to be a Big Man on Campus. At the time I felt quite successful." At least he felt successful until he checked out his values and found that what was important to him didn't count for anything with God! God cares about our character and our love.

So values, and the resultant motives, are crucial. "You don't get what you want," the Bible says, "because you don't ask God for it. And when you do ask he doesn't give it to you, for you ask in quite the wrong spirit—you want only to satisfy your own desires" (James 4:2-3). But God didn't create us and redeem us so we could become self-centered and self-satisfying. His plan for us is holiness. No, not that negative I-don't-do-this-kind-of-thing that we often think of, but the exciting, positive "like God" life that holiness means in Scripture.

If we expect to know God's guidance, we need to be willing to overhaul our values and to grab hold of what's important to God and make it our own. If we aren't willing to accept and live by His values, we earn the biblical description: "You are like unfaithful wives, flirting with the glamour of this world, and never realizing that to be the world's lover means becoming the enemy of God! Anyone who deliberately chooses to be the world's friend is thereby making himself God's enemy" (James 4:4). We have to make a choice. We can't serve two masters.

So until we make this basic choice, all our talk about "knowing God's will" is empty. We've proven unwilling to do what we *do* know. Why should He show us any more?

Means. This is important too. Doing things God's way. "If you really love me," Christ said, "you will keep the commandments I have given you." And He goes on: "Every man who knows my commandments and obeys them is the man who really loves me, and every man who really loves me will himself be loved by my Father, and I too will love him and make myself known to him" (John 14:15, 21).

Put bluntly, this means if you want to sense Christ's hand guiding you, obey Him. If you step outside the biblical rules for living, you step out of intimate contact with God. He won't run after you, begging you to come back so He can guide you. But He will wait for you. And when you're obedient, He'll show you more about His way.

God's means do work out for His best, and we need to be willing to go it His way. Like this seventeen-year-old daughter of missionary parents: "I was trying to decide whether or not to dance and to attend movies. After

praying and reading a lot on both subjects I decided that
they were all right in one area. I, on my own, decided not
to partake in dancing because I feel that too much of the
dancing today is done in a situation and way to arouse
sexual feeling. As a Christian teenager I don't feel this
would be right for me. In the matter of movies I don't feel
that the Lord was telling me that I couldn't attend. So I
told my parents how I felt about it. However, as long as I
am under their care and guidance I will abide by their
rules. I don't see anything wrong with movies if you are
selective in your choice of which you can see."

This girl may miss a few movies by doing things God's
way and respecting the authority of her parents, but she'll
feel good about herself and her maturity. Better still, she
won't miss out on anything God has planned for her. As
we've said, God doesn't plan our lives so we can do everything we want to do, right now. He has a different
purpose. "Everything that happens," the Bible says, "fits
into a pattern for good. God, in his foreknowledge, chose
them [those who love God] to bear the family likeness of
his Son" (Rom. 8:28). Doing things God's way means that
our every experience will help us become more and more
like His Son.

And, to God, that's important.

Many of the decisions we face will be settled quickly if
we take these first two things seriously. But sometimes we
need to add another ingredient to the situation.

Confidence. This is the third ingredient. Or maybe it
would be better to call it "faith." I mean that sense of
certainty one of the kids in this chapter talked about when
she wrote, after praying and thinking about a decision
she had to make, "I was certain and peaceful about it."

A North Carolina girl put it this way: "God has made
—created—each individual. I have come to realize that

since God did make me what I am, He knows me and understands me far better than I can understand myself. So, why not let Him make the decision? He certainly knows what is best for me and how I can find happiness and peace."

This doesn't mean she refuses to accept responsibility for her life, or that she just drifts. It means that she expects God to act as a Person, to let her know what His choice is, and she then expects to do what He chooses. How is she going to know? That's hard to pinpoint. Except that a person whose values are squared away, and who is living an obedient life close to God, will know. As Jesus called Himself our "shepherd," He described His guiding ministry in these words: "He calls his own sheep by name and leads them . . . he goes in front of them himself, and the sheep follow him because they know his voice" (John 10:3*b*-4). Jesus isn't limited. He can and will find ways to let us hear His voice. And when we hear it, we'll recognize it.

Often His voice comes through others, such as parents, church workers (Have you tried talking with your pastor lately?) or school counselors.

Sometimes circumstances are His voice. "When applying to college I naturally had big ideas," says an Illinois college man. "Northwestern, Duke, Wake Forest, etc. But due to my grandmother's incapacity and her being my only relative, it was clear that I'd have to stay close by. I left everything in the Lord's hands because I knew from past experience He would show me what to do. It was a real comedown when He led me to a city junior college where I stayed for a year and a half. It's quite clear now why the Lord did this, because it resolved a lot of questions and was preparing me more fully for the future. My attitude was greatly affected during this period." And so anything in life—our finances, our relatives, our interests, open or closed doors—can be signs of God's leading.

And God will interpret them for us. "I have found now that my only reliance can be on God," says another collegian who asked God to help her understand her circumstances. "This has been true in the question of going to college. Everyone and everything was against my going, except God and His control over me spiritually. And I have found now that this decision was definitely right. The whole 'me' now agrees with this."

Perhaps this is the ultimate indication. The whole "me" agrees. I feel confident that this is His voice.

That's really the great thing about being a Christian. When we have a tough decision to make, we can face it confidently—confident enough to step out and try whatever He directs; to go wherever He leads. "I was debating about doing missionary work overseas last summer," writes a Michigan girl. "I felt inadequate in myself, but I could see that God wanted me to make myself available. At first I thought I was making a big sacrifice, but it was one of the most rewarding summers I've ever spent."

What God wants, we can do.

And maybe this is the key in experiencing God's leading: being willing. Following that biblical advice, "Whatsoever He says to you to do, do it."

Important? It's crucial.

Especially if another Michigan girl is right when she says, "The most important thing is the confidence that *right now* you are in God's will."

Steps to take

1. Do you agree with the author that "knowing God's will" relates to the here and now, and not to

His long-range plan for your life? Why, or why not?

2. If you are uncertain about anything you're presently doing, where do you think the source of the problem probably lies?
   values and motives?
   means?
   confidence?
   What do you think it would take to give you the confidence that *right now*, you are in God's will?

3. If you would like a more detailed description of how to make a decision under God's personal guidance, see chapter 9 of the book *How to Be Real*.

10

Prior commitment

"When I came to Faith Academy," says a fifteen-year-old guy from Texas, "I had to decide whether I would go in the same way I was going in before, or change (for the better). I hadn't really followed as close to God as I should have. I was very wild—my parents couldn't make me do anything. However, I am very glad I took the better road. My decision was one of serving the Lord or just pretending."

We all come to that place sometime where we realize that we have to decide. All of life stretches out before us, filled with thousands of decisions and hundreds of possibilities. To have any control over the kind of life we'll have calls for a prior commitment.

"I've made no real important decisions," says a seventeen-year-old guy from Illinois. "Nothing except whether to try out for sports, and school activities, jobs, etc. None that will affect my future life yet, except maybe college decisions." It might seem that way, but it isn't true. For the little decisions we make every day blend together into the pattern of our life. And that pattern is important. That pattern is *us!*

Take a look at the pattern and you can discover your real values—the "What's important to me?" that underlies your motives and your choices. Take a look at the pattern and you can also discover your idea of what life is all about, your concept of what's in it for you. No, whenever a person thinks that he's made no real important decisions, it only shows that he's not aware of decisions he has already made! It shows he has never consciously come to grips with the meaning of life, and that he's drifting.

Sometimes the littlest thing can jolt us out of that kind of stupor. A decision that doesn't seem all that big can help us break through to the real issue. It happened to one Virginia girl: "I made a decision that all movies were wrong (I've changed my mind since). I decided this because I felt it was hurting myself and others to go to the movies, and I thought I was displeasing the Lord in my attendance. Even though I've changed my mind regarding the decision, it set a precedent in my life to try to make decisions according to the Lord's will, and to think of others, not just myself." It didn't take a "big" decision for her. Just making a little one helped her discover that life demands prior commitment, that life asks us to *decide* what's going to take first place.

This is the question we're all being asked. What is going to take first place in my life? "I had to make a decision if I should be a good Christian or if I should go where the world goes," says a sophomore from Washington state. "Jesus came into my life at age twelve, and I will never be sorry, because I've seen my best friends and how many problems they have. I learned to know Jesus as a personal Friend and Person who I can talk to at any time and tell my problems to. My God is wonderful!

"I think," she goes on, "something should be said about how your decisions will be easier when you have Jesus Christ in your life." Others agreed. Like the collegian who said, "Before one can focus on values, he must focus on Jesus Christ. Until we know Him *personally,* values have no meaning."

You probably know what they're talking about. The best news in the world is that Jesus Christ offers to step into our lives, to reshape our personalities and our perspectives, and to share His own vital life with us. Personal relationship with Jesus Christ *is* first, for only in knowing Him can we begin to see life from God's viewpoint. So any person who is consciously sifting his values, aware that it's time to make a commitment to a way of life, does need to check out his relationship with God first. He needs to be sure that he hasn't just *heard* of Christ's death for sinners, but that he has made it personal, and by faith accepted the forgiveness God offers all who trust Him.

But this is still only a first step. Becoming a Christian doesn't make life fall into place automatically. "My hang-up," says a Christian guy, "came in actually standing for what I knew. Young people (as well as everyone) need the self-discipline and determination to uphold their values and what they know to be right. This was always my problem—not in knowing right from wrong or the proper or wise values, but sticking by what I believed. The influence of the peer group and the standards of the society are often very hard to overcome." What he needed was *commitment*.

This is what the Bible says too. "Your goodness must be accompanied by knowledge, your knowledge by self-control, your self-control by the ability to endure. Your endurance too must always be accompanied by devotion to God; that in turn must have in it the quality of brotherliness, and your brotherliness must lead on to Christian love. If you have these qualities existing and growing in you then it means that knowing our Lord Jesus Christ has not made your lives either complacent or unproductive. The man whose life fails to exhibit these qualities is shortsighted—he can no longer see the reason why he was cleansed from his former sins" (2 Peter 1:5-9).

Becoming a Christian isn't the end. It's the beginning of a life that is to have unique qualities "existing and grow-

ing." And this calls for each Christian to commit himself
to live by God's values.

Eyes wide open

Buying all of God's values isn't something we ought to
do blindfolded. We ought to look at competing ideas
about life—like the ones discussed in the first few chapters. And we ought to check out God's Big Picture, and
His revealed purpose for individuals. Then, as the Bible
says, "with eyes wide open" we can decide. What kind of
decision does the Bible call for? Paul puts it this way: "I
beg you, my brothers, as an act of intelligent worship, to
give him your bodies, as a living sacrifice, consecrated to
him and acceptable by him. Don't let the world squeeze
you into its own mold, but let God remold your minds
from within, so that you may prove in practice that the
plan of God for you is good, meets all his demands and
moves toward the goal of true maturity" (Rom. 12:1-2).

As an "*intelligent* act" this kind of commitment invites
us to come to our own conclusions about the meaning of
life. God actually wants us to decide for ourselves what
we want in life, and what life means. But if we decide His
view is right, then we're to follow through with an "intelligent *act*." You are to "put yourself in God's hands as
weapons of good for his own purposes" (Rom. 6:12).

We all have this decision to make, even if life only
seems to be made up of little things. Will I or won't I
commit my life to God to be lived His way? Will I or won't
I live as a new person "who is out to learn what he ought
to be, according to the plan of God" (Col. 3:10)?

What will an "I will" commitment mean? Happiness?
Not necessarily. But meaning, a sense of purpose, an
inner joy, a confident peace, a solid hope, and the expec-
tation of an exciting future—it will mean all of this.

As for us, an "I will" commitment means accepting new responsibilities. It means looking at life from God's viewpoint, searching the Scriptures daily to discover what's important to Him, and then acting in faith on what we learn.

It means living by these values.

No matter what.

Steps to take

1. How would you answer the question if someone asked you about life and said, "What's in it for me?"

2. Jesus said something striking on this commitment theme. What do you think He meant by this: "If anyone wants to follow in my footsteps he must give up all right to himself, take up his cross and follow me. For the man who wants to save his life will lose it; but the man who loses his life for my sake will find it" (Matt. 16:24-25).

    What do you think this means?

    What does it mean *to you*?

Notes

Chapter 1

[1]About 2,000 young people in high school and college shared their ideas and experiences to help produce this book. All the quotes are authentic—printed just the way real people said or wrote them.

Chapter 2

[1]Milton Rokeach, *Beliefs, Attitudes and Values* (San Francisco: Jossy-Bass, 1968), p. 160.

[2]Grace and Fred Hechinger, *Teen-age Tyranny* (New York: Morrow, 1963), p. 204.

[3]James S. Coleman, *The Adolescent Society* (New York: Free Press of Glencoe, 1961), p. 37.

Chapter 3

[1]John E. Horrocks, "Adolescent Attitudes and Goals" in Muzafer Sherif and C. W. Sherif, eds., *Problems of Youth* (Chicago: Aldine, 1965), p. 21.

[2]Merton F. Strommer, *Profiles of Church Youth* (St. Louis: Concordia, 1963), p. 72.

Chapter 4

[1]Merton F. Strommer, *Profiles of Church Youth* (St. Louis: Concordia, 1963), p. 76.

[2]Ibid., p. 85.

[3]William C. Kvaraceus, *Dynamics of Delinquency* (New York: Merrill Books, 1966), p. 35.

Chapter 5

[1]Karl C. Garrison, *Psychology of Adolescence* (6th ed.; Englewood Cliffs, N.J.: Prentice-Hall, 1964), p. 183.

[2]Corlis Lamont, *The Philosophy of Humanism* (New York: Fred. Ungar, 1965), p. 227.

[3]Ibid.

[4]Ibid., p. 3.

Chapter 7

[1]I'm taking it for granted that you and I are pretty close on our view of the Bible and our conviction that God communicates with us in it. If you have some questions about this, or some doubts about God and your relationship to Him, you might be interested in another book, *How I Can Experience God.*

[2]An important one is described in chapter 8 of the book *How I Can Be Real.*

Chapter 8

[1]Allen J. Moore, *The Youth Adult Generation* (Nashville: Abingdon, 1969), p. 50.

[2]James S. Coleman, *The Adolescent Society* (New York: Free Press of Glencoe, 1961), p. 291.